INNER
life

David Torkington has sold over 400,000 books and been translated into 13 languages.

BOOKS BY DAVID TORKINGTON

The Primacy of Loving – The Spirituality of the Heart

*Wisdom from The Christian Mystics –
How to Pray the Christian Way*

Wisdom from the Western Isles – The Making of a Mystic

Wisdom from Franciscan Italy – The Primacy of Love

How to Pray – A Practical Guide to the Spiritual Life

Prayer Made Simple – CTS booklet

Inner Life – A Fellow Traveller's Guide to Prayer

A New Beginning – A Sideways Look at the Spiritual Life

Dear Susanna – It's Time for a Christian Renaissance

His website is https://www.davidtorkington.com

INNER
life

A Fellow Traveller's Guide to Prayer

DAVID TORKINGTON

Foreword by Sister Wendy Beckett

Essentialist Press

First published in 1997 by Darton, Longman and Todd, Ltd.
1 Spencer Court, 140-142 Wandsworth High Street, London SW18 411

The right of David Torkington to be identified as the author of this work has been asserted in accordance with the Copyright, Designs and Patents Act 1988.

Torkington, David.

Inner life: a fellow traveller's guide to prayer/ David Torkington.

Cover design by The Sisters at the Benedictines of Mary, Queen of Apostles

Original ISBN: 0-8189-0818-1

Paperback ISBN 979-8-9895293-3-9

Hardcover ISBN 979-8-9895293-4-6

eBook ISBN 979-8-9895293-4-6

©Copyright 1997 David Torkington

Foreword © 1997 Sr. Wendy Beckett

No part of this book may be reproduced, stored in a retrieval system, or transmitted in any form, or by any means, electronic, mechanical, photocopying, or otherwise, without the prior written permission of the publisher, except by a reviewer, who may quote brief passages in a review.

Essentialist Press

ESSENTIALIST
PRESS

Coeur d'Alene, ID 83815

www.EssentialistPress.com

This book is dedicated to Fr Francis Handley who first taught me how to pray.

Contents

Foreword 1

The Authors preface to the second edition of 'Inner Life' 2

1
The happiest day of my Life 6

2
First recollections 9

3
Bargaining with God 12

4
From Toy Town with love 15

5
A meeting on the moor 18

6
Brahms and beyond 21

7
The perfect icon 24

8
Fear and fascination 27

9
Converging streams 30

10
St Martin Buber 33

11
A powerful magnetic force 36

12
New horizons 39

13 A spiritual lifeline	42
14 The empty tomb	45
15 The present continuing tense	49
16 Drop out, turn on, tune in	52
17 Spirituality from the "kitsch 'n sink"	55
18 Familiarity breeds conceit	58
19 Thank God for being God	61
20 Power in weakness	64
21 Actions speak louder than words	67
22 Into another dimension	70
23 The only magic that matters	73
24 The whole truth and nothing but the truth	76
25 The Feel-Good Factor	79
26 The one thing necessary	82
27 Who wins a rat-race?	85
28 Schola Divini Amoris	88

29
Walking the tightrope... 91

30
The Secret of Success.. 94

31
Blind love.. 98

32
Love in Lourdes.. 101

33
Thanks to my lucky stars 104

34
When sparks first flicker into flame............................... 107

35
The fallen idol 110

36
Into the dark night 113

37
The Cloud of Understanding 116

38
The prayer of incompetence 119

39
The enemy within.. 122

40
The prayer of the heart 125

41
Philokalia.. 128

42
In extremis 131

43
Preaching to the converted 134

44
The prayer for all times 137

Chapter 45
In perfect harmony... 140

46
An oasis in the desert... 143

Chapter 47
Hide-and-seek... 146

48
The Rambo within... 149

49
Spiritual paternity... 152

50
The spiritual combat.. 155

51
True wisdom.. 158

52
From stumbling blocks to stepping stones........................ 161

Foreword

For spiritual writings, there is only one test. It is not whether they sound impressive; style matters, and David Torkington writes with admirable clarity, but this is only a means, and can be used to self-glorying ends. Nor is the test whether our hearts are touched. This too matters, but emotions are volatile. The only real test is whether what is written makes us love God more. Put in another way, the test is practical, not whether we feel we love him more but whether we lay down the book — or the Catholic Herald, that noble publication in which these pieces first appeared — and begin to consider what we must do.

It is all in the doing, that resolute activity that turns our vague longings into practice, and that is something Torkington profoundly understands. It is so easy to read spirituality and, in the reading, deceive ourselves into thinking we live it. This book leaves us no bolt hole for self-deception. Torkington does not speak to us from a lofty pinnacle of achievement. He does not talk down: he is already down, there on the plateau with us poor stragglers, inspiring us to hold out to Jesus our wretchedness, our lack of love, so that his own Yes to the Father may be spoken within our hearts. Torkington is concerned with the reality of love, its failures, its desires, its need to trust and let Jesus take possession. He is absolutely certain that we cannot do it, but that God can, and in communicating that certainty, so humbly and so surely, he gives us confidence to turn the floating desire for God that all humans have, into prayer and acts of goodness.

This is a rare and wonderful gift. It is pure bonus that Torkington, who always starts from life as it is lived, is also an interesting writer. One can imagine an atheist or an agnostic enjoying this book for its literary appeal and then the true meaning sinking in and torpedoing the faithlessness (innocent faithlessness, of course!). For those to whom God has already given the grace of believing, all this book will torpedo is our complacency, our lethargy and our reluctance to let God love us and make us loving in return. It should be mandatory reading!

Sister Wendy Beckett

The Author's preface to the second edition of 'Inner Life'

When this book was first published in 1997, conventual wisdom believed that 2,000 books had to be sold for the publisher to be in the black. Although this book quickly achieved this objective the original publisher decided that it only reached those goals because at the time, I was a popular columnist in the Catholic Herald. They did not feel that outside this following there was sufficient interest in prayer to guarantee the publication of another 2000 copies. The book therefore went out of print. Recent events in the Church however have led many to rightly believe that only God can reverse a trend at the highest level that is leading the majority into heresy on a scale not seen since Arianism fifteen hundred years ago.

That is why once again people are turning to prayer because prayer is merely the word that is used to describe how we turn to God so that he can once more destroy a heresy or heresies that abound today through those who welcome him into their lives.

The approach to prayer is unique because instead of merely detailing the authentic Catholic prayer tradition, I have instead explained that tradition in a series of short autobiographical essays that I originally hoped would both amuse and edify the reader. Naturally I have re-edited them to make each essay more accessible to a contemporary reader, however, they are essentially the same essays that I wrote almost thirty years ago. Each starts at the very beginning of prayer or at least of my prayer life, and the stories progress to the very height of what St Teresa of Avila would call the Mystical Marriage in her masterwork 'The Interior Castle'.

The 'Essentialist Press' has recently been founded to produce books that deal with matters of serious concern in both the religious and secular world, by recruiting writers whose expertise in their respective fields of competence is all but unrivalled. I was therefore deeply moved to be asked to write for them to detail the God-given spirituality that Christ introduced into early Christianity, that is now sadly being undermined today at the very highest level in the Church.

In particular, I wanted to detail the profound prayer lives that this spirituality inculcated into every early Christian, because this too has all but disappeared when compared to the living and vital prayer life that animated the first Christians. Such a prayer life enabled them to transform an ancient pagan Empire into a Christian Empire in such a short time, promising that what was once done in the past can be done again today.

All that is needed is the Holy Spirit. The same Holy Spirit that has never deserted us in spite of us deserting him by failing to develop the only form of deep prayer that can enable Him to change our world through us.

In the last thirty years I have written over ten books developing this theme. However, on rereading *Inner Life – A Fellow Traveller's Guide to Prayer* I have been amazed to discover that, after all the other books that I have written, that may well go wider and deeper into the development of prayer, this book is the simplest and the most reader-friendly of them all. It is the book that I would give above all the others that I have written to the person who asks the question, "Please tell me how I should pray." This is probably because it contains within it my own personal journey enabling the reader to identify with my journey and so encourage them to press on in their own. This is particularly true because, after travelling on, or rather in 'The Way' for more than fifty years I have been able to see how the journey unfolds in a way that is not open to the beginner. It is this perhaps above all that makes it into the perfect, "Fellow Traveller's Guide to Prayer".

If you know exactly where you are going and the pleasures and pitfalls along the way, then that Way become far more attainable. Since this book went out of print, I have seen the first editions offered for sale on Amazon for between $40 and $400 because it has been so difficult to get a hold of. I am delighted therefore that the 'Essentialist Press' is republishing this book at an easily affordable price to hopefully lead you, the reader, into greater union with God.

Fraternally,

David Torkington

1

The happiest day of my Life

I was told my First Holy Communion Day would be the happiest day of my life. I found it difficult to believe that it could be happier than Christmas day or bonfire night, or a day out at the fun fair, but I was prepared to keep an open mind. Then someone told me that God would grant any prayer, any request that you made of him if it was made while the sacred host was actually in your mouth and on your tongue, as long as you didn't touch it with your teeth. Naturally that made all the difference, all the difference in the world.

I began to prepare myself for the big day by visiting the local sports shop to gaze at the bicycle of my dreams that God was going to give me on the happiest day of my life. When I told Miss Holt, our teacher, what I was going to ask for she told me that God may not think it would be good for me, and he did try to give priority to unselfish little boys who asked for things for others. So, I decided to pray for my brother instead. He suffered with polio when he was six and wore an iron caliper and a built-up boot ever since.

When the day came, the moment I got back to my place I closed my eyes, clasped my hands together and asked God to make Peter's leg better. I was sure he would answer my prayer, especially as I gave up the bicycle of my dreams. I remember my disappointment when I came out of Mass and saw my brother still hobbling about

1 - The happiest day of my Life

with his stick in his hand. I was so sure I would be given something special on my First Communion Day and instead I nearly lost my faith. It was the first time I had to face up to the problem of unanswered prayer, but it was not the last.

We all begin by trying to manipulate God to get what we want out of him, and then get upset when we can't, or blame him for not caring for us as he should, or even doubting that he is there at all. Do you remember that awful horror story about the monkey's paw, and the three wishes that caused hell on earth for the man who thought they would make him happy forever? It is a cautionary tale for all who think that getting what you want out of God will make you happy. Who was it who said, "If you want to make a person miserable then give them everything they ask for?"

The real problem is not with God; it is with us. He is full of selflessness and wants the best for everyone. We are full of selfishness and don't know what is good for anyone. Take my brother as a case in point. He was mad on sports.

He loved rugby and cricket and athletics even though for the most part he had to be satisfied with watching others do what he would love to do himself. At first it made him frustrated and angry, but when he learned to accept his weakness, it was his very weakness that enabled him to come close to God. When he died at the age of twenty-two he had come as close to God as anyone I had ever known.

Hundreds of people came to his funeral and scores of them said what a good man he was and how good he was to them personally. Many people said they were so inspired by his simple goodness that he changed the whole course of their lives. If I had my way he might have played for his county at cricket, even played for his country at rugby or achieved a gold medal at the Olympics, but he would not have been a tenth of the man he was when he died.

The reason why it would be disastrous if we were always given what we wanted when we prayed, is that selfishness is so deeply rooted in us all that we do not really know what we do want, but God does. Deep down beyond all the petty things we pray for and think are so important, the one thing we want above everything else is "everything." God is everything we want, and we will only be happy when we have him. I'm not saying that we shouldn't pray for little things, even big things, for ourselves and for others, because on some occasions our requests will be answered — God knows why!

But one thing's for sure, prayer will always be answered because it is always a sign that we know how weak we are, how much in need we are, and how deep down behind all the selfishness that drives us all, we dearly want the only one who can give us everything that we really do want. We start our prayer journey by trying to use God, trying to exploit him, and as we keep on trying he gradually teaches us that in the end it is he who wants to exploit us. He will if we persevere, even if we persevere in praying for the wrong things. But he wants to exploit us for ourselves so that we can become our true selves by being filled to overflowing with the fullness of life and love that we've longed for from the very beginning but have been too blind to see it. Thank God for God!

2

First recollections

My first recollections of prayer were of kneeling at my bedside repeating the self-same set of petitions night after night. God bless Mummy and Daddy, Tony, and Peter, and all my aunts and uncles who were mentioned by name. It was only after all my cousins were prayed for, in order of age, that my turn came. I was taught not to ask God to bless me as he was asked to bless everyone else but to make me a good boy! Who wants to be a good boy? I never did. I wanted to be like my heroes from *Just William*. I bet William didn't pray "Please God make me a good boy," and I bet Ginger didn't either, and I'm positive Violet Elizabeth Bott didn't pray to be made a good girl.

So, I stopped praying to be made a good boy the moment I was left to pray on my own, and I started to ask for things instead. The first time I stormed the gates of heaven it was to ask for either an airgun or a catapult. Nothing happened for about a week, and I was just about to lapse into atheism when the parish priest told the whole school that God was not only everywhere but knew everything, even our most secret thoughts.

It did not take me long to rumble why my weapons of destruction had not materialized. If God knew all things, even my most secret thoughts, he knew what I wanted them for. From then on I stopped praying for things as often as I would have liked. Most things I wanted did not somehow fit in with being a good boy, so I didn't think God would be the best person to ask. Instead, I asked Father Christmas. When he turned out to be a hoax I turned back to God again, but knowing he knew everything made me think twice before asking him for anything but spiritual things, except when the bus didn't turn up, or the school report was about to arrive, or I lost something valuable.

When I look back, my spiritual life seems to have gone up and down and round and round like a roller-coaster at a fairground. When I was up I was too busy enjoying myself to think of God and when I was down I prayed desperately to be up again. Who could blame God if he became fed up with people like me. The truth is I became fed up with myself, so fed up and so ashamed of myself that even when I was down and everything seemed to be going wrong, pride regularly prevented me from crying out for the help I needed.

I sometimes had to hit rock bottom before I found the humility to start asking for help. When I was working in Africa I started asking St. Jude to help me out. He is very big in Africa, probably because they are in such obvious physical need that they are not ashamed to make the patron of hopeless cases their favorite saint. I know some people do not like the idea of asking the saints for help. I was not keen on the idea myself once, and I don't do it much now, but quite apart from anything else, it indicates a person's humility. It is an awareness of our own weakness, so aware that we turn to someone else to ask on our behalf, someone much better and much holier than we are.

Everyone knows that it is God in the end who hears prayer and answers it, but asking for the help of someone else reveals a measure of the humility that must accompany any genuine cry for help. It helps to ask friends to pray for us too, and for the same reason. It is one thing to admit to ourselves our own weaknesses and our own needs in private, but it takes humility a step further when we make them public by asking others to pray for us. So, the real importance of asking someone to pray for us, whether it is one of the saints, a friend or even a passing acquaintance, is that it demonstrates to God that humility is beginning to outbalance the pride that always keeps him at bay.

St Padre Pio was once asked by one of his brothers to pray for him because he was in such need. Knowing that the friar was better at asking others to do what he would not do for himself, St Padre Pio simply said, "No! My prayer will not do you any good if you do not pray for yourself." You can enlist the whole communion of saints and all the choirs of angels and the whole of the church militant to pray for you if you like, but it will not do you any good, if you do not pray for yourself.

I met a very holy man once who lived in a cave at the top of Mount Alverna in Tuscany and I asked him to pray for me, especially when I was spiritually down and out. Without any hesitation he said, "No! You pray for yourself, and God will hear you. I will pray for you when everything is going well. That is when you will really be in need of help." St. John of the Cross used to say that when we are feeling down in the dumps and it seems God is a million miles away, we are usually closer to him than when we are feeling on top of the world. He said we are safer then. Danger begins when we are feeling better because we usually feel we can get on very well by ourselves, thank you very much!

I suppose the moral of all this is that we should pray always, when we are up and when we are down, but especially when we are up, enlisting all the help we can. Then God can gradually build us up into the person he wants us to become from the ruins that we are at the beginning of our journey.

3

Bargaining with God

I was never happy to be anything less than number one, so you can imagine how I felt when Miss Holt made me number two for the big day. And what was worse, I was number two to a girl! When I sulked, it was explained to me that everyone would laugh if I was made the May Queen, so I had no choice but to accept my role as a trainbearer with five other boys.

The only way I could get my own back on my favorite teacher was by wolfing a large slice of chocolate cake that she forbade us to touch until after the crowning. She thought the handkerchief I held to my face had been used to wipe away tears instead of the incriminating evidence that collected around my mouth, so she gave me a velvet cushion and made me crown-bearer to the queen.

I made the mistake of sitting next to the radiator when the visiting preacher began his interminable sermon. Before he was more than halfway through, the chocolate cake began to cook inside my stomach, and I have never been particularly fond of hot chocolate pudding. It ended up on the caretaker's compost heap long before the sermon was over, and I ended up feeling sicker than I had ever felt before.

It was the first time I really prayed. Oh, I did say prayers before with my mother at bedtime, and I recited them too at school as-

3 - Bargaining with God

sembly, but this was the first time I really meant what I said. I can remember my prayer quite clearly to this day. "Please, God, make me better, and I'll never be a naughty boy again."

Even at that tender age I realized that God could not be bribed, not even with the whole contents of my piggy bank, not even with the contents of all the piggy banks in the whole world. God had everything he wanted, everything that money could buy. But I discovered that I had it in my power to give God something that money could not buy, something that Miss Holt had said God wanted more than anything else. He wanted me to be a "good boy." If I could promise that to God, then I would be able to get whatever I wanted out of him.

I lay in bed the next morning with a feeling of power that I never felt before. I knew I could always get round Miss Holt whenever I wanted but now I had found out how to get round God! In case God rumbled my little game I only asked him when things were desperate, and even then I tried to be a little better for a day or two as insurance for the future.

I came across a book on prayer recently which said that the first heartfelt prayer we ever make is usually the prayer of bargaining with God, offering our good behavior in return for his good will. It went on to say that it is almost the last prayer we make too, when we see death approaching. It is then that we offer, as we have never offered before, to live a better life on earth in exchange for a wonderful life in heaven, a life that does not seem half as certain or half as wonderful when it is only a few heartbeats away.

It made me realize just how much old habits die hard, for the habit I learned as a small child remained with me throughout my adolescence into my adult life, and in fact has stayed with me to this day. I am all too ready to get hot under the collar when I read or hear about bribery in commercial life or in political life, but truth to tell, I have been blind to the bribery in my own spiritual life.

I have spent most of my life trying to bribe God, to make him bend his will to my will instead of mine to his. The book I mentioned earlier said that when, as death approaches, we realize that God cannot be bribed, and we do at last what we should have done at first. We surrender our will to his will. The peace that can so often be seen in those who are about to die is the direct result of this surrender to the will of God. It is a peace that surpasses the understanding of those whose prayer life never develops beyond that of a merchant bargaining in the marketplace.

If only we could learn at the beginning of our lives what so many learn only at the end of their lives, we might find sooner than we think the peace that we desire above all else, for ourselves and for the world we live in.

4

From Toy Town with love

I was brought up on the radio, or the wireless as we called it. I used to ache for children's hour to begin. It would transport me into another world. One of my favorite other worlds was "Toy Town" and my favorite character was Larry the Lamb. He was always getting himself into trouble, yet he was always well-mannered and respectful. It was always, "Please Mr. Policeman, Sir" and "Please Mr. Mayor." I don't know who wrote the script, but the writer knew a lot about children and how they are more interested in what a person does than in what a person is. If a man was always grumbling then he was "Mr Grouser." If he could perform tricks he was "Mr Magician" and if he made things he was "Mr Inventor."

We used to have a picture of the Sacred Heart at home and when my mother explained who he was and what the flames around his heart meant, I remember pointing and saying, "It's Mr. Loving!" I could not have been more than about five or six at the time. It was the first theological statement I ever made and it made everyone laugh. But the parish priest did not laugh. He said I was quite right and asked my parents who taught me to say that Jesus was "Mr Loving." They were completely nonplussed and said they had no idea. "Where did you hear that Jesus was Mr. Loving?" asked Fr Wilkin. "Who told you to call him that?" "I just looked at the ground in front of me and said nothing. It was my secret and in any case, I did not want to disappoint him by telling him that I heard about it from "Toy Town" and Larry the Lamb, and I certainly did not want everyone to laugh at me again.

Years later when I began to study the Scriptures, I was told that the Jews, unlike the Greeks, were existentialists. They were like children, not so much interested in what a person is, but in what a person does. God is not just love, but God is loving, and he is loving all the time, so Larry the Lamb was right after all, and so was I. The Sacred Heart is Mr Loving and that is why the devotion grew up in the first place at a time when everyone had been taught to believe that God was Mr Policeman. The statues once common in all our churches and the pictures to be found in most Catholic homes were meant to be a continual reminder of the most important truth of our faith, and it is this. God is not just love but loving, and he is loving us all the time.

I must admit that when I began to study the new theology at the time of Vatican II, I became a spiritual snob and began to look down on the simple faith that I was brought up on, on the devotions that once sustained me. My artistic sensibilities were offended by those ghastly plaster statues of the Sacred Heart and the other dreadful pictures that most Catholics used to hang in their homes with pride. For many years I studied the origins of the Liturgical Movement and the Paschal mystery became the center of the new spirituality that sustained me. I began to understand the meaning and importance of the Resurrection as never before. It is not just a great historical event that happened two thousand years ago, it is an event that is happening now. Jesus is risen now! He is alive now, and the same power, the same love, that raised him from the dead is accessible now to all who would receive it, to do in us what has already been done in Jesus.

It took me many more years to realize that as T.S. Eliot wrote, "The end of all our journeying is to end up at the place where we started and to know that place for the first time." The wonderful truths that I learned from my study of the new theology were not new at all. I was brought up on them as were my parents and their parents before them. The plaster statue of "Mr Loving" may be a little old-fashioned by today's standards, and the pictures that used to be so common in our homes may not be as acceptable today as they were in the past. But the truth behind the devotion to the Sacred Heart is the most important truth of our faith, and that truth is timeless. Who is the Sacred Heart but Jesus risen from the dead? He is represented not just as Love Incarnate but as Incarnate Loving. He is "Mr Loving."

I think I could identify with my friend from "Toy Town" so easily because he was always bleating, "I'm only a little lamb!" and I was only a little boy! I might not have been able to turn to Mr Policeman or Mr Inventor or Mr Magician whenever I needed help, but I could always turn to Mr Loving instead, who was more than all of them rolled into one.

When little lambs grow up they can sometimes become too independent for their own good and so can little boys. That is why I'm not ashamed to admit that all my journeying has brought me back to the place where I first started, and I now know the place for the first time. Nor am I ashamed to admit that my first spiritual inspiration came from a lamb, Larry the Lamb, from "Toy Town."

5

A meeting on the moor

I went up to London to spend Christmas with friends and saw over a dozen kestrels searching for their Christmas dinner along the motorways. They reminded me of the first kestrel I ever saw, high up on the Yorkshire moors just below Ingleborough, where we used to spend our summer holidays during the war.

Kestrels were comparatively rare in those days, at least to a townie like me, so I watched it for hours hunting in the heather. I loved the peat moorland and the height of Ingleborough towering over our little cottage. No other landscape has ever affected me more deeply, perhaps because it was my first love and there is always something special, something uniquely precious about your first love.

I loved that land where my forebears had lived for generations before me, but it was only on that day as I gazed in wonder at the "windhover" balancing on high that I knew it loved me in a way I found hard to explain to anyone; so, I didn't try. The further the kestrel floated away on the wind the smaller it became, and the more it drew me together within myself and made me ever more open and sensitive to the landscape over which it soared.

From the beginning, contemplatives have always found that some sort of fixed point, real or imagined, can help concentrate the mind

5 - A meeting on the moor

and heart on what they desire more than anything else. I suppose this was the first "natural" mystical experience I ever had, though I did not quite know what it was at the time. I just knew I wanted more of it but found to my great disappointment that it was even rarer than the bird that had drawn me out of myself.

I do not want to give the impression that my youth was strewn with "mystical experiences" because it was not, but they did come to me frequently enough to make me wonder and pause to reflect on their meaning. I thought they were unique to me at first and my religious upbringing made me associate the profound feeling that enveloped me with the One whose Spirit hovered over the chaos at the dawn of time and whose Word formed it into the paradise on earth that mirrored the paradise in heaven. If the world was formed by his Word at the beginning of time, could it not speak to people of every time and fill them with the Spirit who still hovers over it, as the hawk that hovers on high?

Gradually I came to realize that the experience I had on the moor was not unique to me but was a commonplace experience of all humankind who learn how to be still and know their Creator through the creation that embodies his Word. At first, I thought my experience spoke to me of a special calling, perhaps to become a priest or a religious, as many others have done, misinterpreting the mysterious touch that calls all to the fulness of love in every way of life.

When I got beyond the stage where I could not talk to my father about anything and began to talk to him about everything, I found he had the same experience that I had in my youth. Then, when he met my mother, he found in her a fuller and more complete embodiment of what I experienced on my beloved moorland.

If creation can speak to us of the goodness, beauty, and truth that it mirrors and reveals to us, how much more can its greatest masterworks? How much more can man and woman, made most particularly in his own image and likeness, speak to each other of the fulness of love that they both reflect in different complementary ways? Only the blindness of pride and prejudice can prevent the would-be mystic from experiencing ever more fully, ever more completely, the otherworldly love that surrounds them. This is why the mystic way, which is the only way to come to know and experience the fulness of love, means sacrifice and involves much purifying suffering Only the pure of heart can see God in the world he created and in the men and women he has formed in his own image and likeness.

If the whole of creation is a sacrament, then marriage is a sacrament par excellence, because it opens to everyone the hope and the opportunity of going beyond themselves through loving sacrifice, not just into each other but into the Other, who is uniquely but differently embodied in each.

Although he is the All in all, he still hovers over all, not like the kestrel that threatens death, but like the dove that promises peace to every genuine searcher whose heart will never rest till it rests in him.

6

Brahms and beyond

I know Christmas is supposed to be a time of peace and goodwill, but I believe more family rows break out at Christmas than at any other time of the year. The first one that I can remember was started by me. My father gave us the choice of the latest three-speed Decca gramophone, or a television and my two older brothers chose the gramophone. How could they possibly choose boring old classical music in preference to "Muffin the Mule," "What's My Line?" and a host of other exciting programs that drew me to the box like a magnet, and led me to make friends with boys I would not normally have passed the time of day with? My musical appreciation had recently risen from "Little Brown Jug" and "The Teddy Bears' Picnic" to the "Thunder and Lightning Polka" so I was hardly in a position to appreciate the complicated music that they seemed to like.

When I was confined to bed with a sore throat for a few days I started thinking. If their sort of music made them turn down a television, which I thought was the only thing worth living for at the time, then there must be something in it. So, I decided to try to find out what it was. When everyone else was out I put on one of their records, the Brahms Double Concerto. After playing it three times and getting nowhere I decided it was not a patch on "Little Brown Jug," or "The Teddy Bears' Picnic" for that matter, but I nevertheless decided to give it one more chance that afternoon, as I had nothing better to do. Fourth time round I began to notice that it did have a few tunes in it after all, and two of them at least were quite nice, so I listened to the second and third movements once more. Then I kept listening to the second movement, until I was hooked.

At first, I just noticed the main theme, then I started to notice what the composer did with it, how he would wrap it up in funny ways that I quite liked and then suddenly reintroduce it when I was least expecting it. It was the beginning of my conversion to classical music. When I listened to the whole work for the last time before going back to school, I found that it was not all headwork, as it had been to begin with, but my heart was touched too, and I became totally absorbed in the music. My heart and mind spiraled upwards with the main theme in the last movement and left me on a sort of spiritual high that did not end with the music.

It was exactly the same experience I had on the Yorkshire moors during my summer holidays when I watched the kestrel hunting in the heather till it soared out of sight. When back at school I was taught that prayer was the raising of the heart and the mind to God, I thought perhaps that this is what I was doing on the moors and while listening to the music that moved me so deeply. Perhaps the experiences I had were genuine experiences of God.

I did not have the courage to ask the priest who taught us catechism because what I experienced was so personal and private, and anyway I did not want the other boys to think I was soft, so I said nothing. When later, I had similar experiences that drew me together and beyond myself, sometimes after intensive study, or a night at the theater or the opera, or even after a particularly inspiring film, I started reading a few books on mystical prayer to see if my intuitions were right and found that they were.

6 - Brahms and beyond

Although these experiences were rare and never predictable, I found they were common to most people, especially in their youth, and were a genuine if brief glimpse of what is called contemplation in the Christian mystical tradition. It seemed that the "real thing" is like a simple semi-hypnotic gaze upon God, accompanied by a certain reverence and awe that raises the whole of the human spirit and makes the receiver not only yearn for more but yearn to do more for the One whose love seems to envelop them.

The rare glimpses that I experienced had all the hallmarks of the "real thing," but were never long enough to do more than make me want to seek out the One whose mystical presence had briefly touched me. Although all I had read made it clear that the way ahead involved a profound and painful purification, I nevertheless decided I wanted to journey on, come what may, into the unknown, where the ultimately unknowable can be known a little more fully.

7

The perfect icon

I could never understand why I was always being blamed for being spoiled just because I was the youngest in the family. After all, it was not my fault I was an afterthought. But blame I got, or so I thought, when anything went wrong, or something could not be found, or when I seemed to be favored over my brothers who were several years older than me. So, I got used to chanting "It's not my fault," not just to absolve me from the latest alleged crime, but for the unforgivable crime of being born the Benjamin of the family. Despite the sin for which there is no forgiveness I knew deep down that it did make me special, and also especially loved, even by the brothers who teased rather than tormented me. But even their special love did not make up for the age gap that made me something of an only child with no one with whom to share my deepest thoughts.

I used to feel aggrieved that I never had long philosophical discussions with them about the "Origins of the Species" or the ultimate destiny of Homo Sapiens, as I fondly imagined other brothers and sisters did. So, it was something of a surprise to learn in later life that neither did they have these discussions with one another. I was more than halfway to middle age before I found out that their spiritual experiences had been similar to mine, that they too had been touched by what had touched me, though each of us had given our

7 - The perfect icon

experiences distinct interpretations that eventually led to different ways of life.

My brother Peter was the artist in the family. He loved nothing better than disappearing for hours on end with his canvas and brushes to paint castles and cathedrals, and then his beloved icons that eventually took over from everything else. In summer he set out for the Peak District on his large three-wheeler, with the tools of his trade strapped on the back and would return radiant to show us other icons, purple mountains, silver streams, and grey granite cliffs with weedy looking trees hanging on for dear life. Then later in the evening I'd often see him gazing into space, mulling over the mysterious touch that made him mourn for his maker.

Although Peter was the only pianist in the family apart from my mother, it was Tony, my eldest brother who turned to music more than anything else for the icons that meant so much to him. Although he loved all classical music, he loved opera more than anything else. He spent hours queuing up to buy tickets for the latest touring company and on one occasion he hitched a lift to London to hear Maria Callas as Norma at The Royal Opera House, Covent Garden. Shortly before he died, I asked him why opera meant so much to him. "It's because I love the human voice," he said, "because in some subtle and miraculous way it is the most moving expression I know of the deepest feelings and emotions of the human spirit."

I have often quoted my brother to soulless sceptics who complain about opera singers spending hours declaring their love for each other or dying with daggers in their hearts. They are so busy mocking what seems to them to be something surreal, that they are blind to the reality, the soul that speaks through music more than through any other medium and more through the human voice than through any other instrument. What Peter experienced through his art, Tony experienced through his music, that made him mourn too for the same mysterious presence that had touched his brother. My brothers' favorite icons finally led them to the Perfect Icon. Peter found his way through poetry, through the romantics and through Gerard Manley Hopkins; Tony through prose, through G.K. Chesterton and his masterly work on St. Francis of Assisi.

I came by way of St. Augustine who was entranced by the same icons that had so moved us whilst he was still a pagan, and then followed them like the wise men before him to the most Perfect Icon of all. In Christ alone can be found all the beauty, all the truth and all the goodness that can only be glimpsed in the rest of creation. But in him everything is brought to perfection and literally embodied so that everybody can find in him the spiritual completion for which their souls have been craving from the beginning. Every serious searcher who has briefly experienced the presence of the All in all for themselves will feel compelled to search on until they discover that nothing but the All himself will satisfy them anymore.

8

Fear and fascination

I was devastated when my father announced that he was going to give up our holiday home in the Yorkshire Dales, but I suppose it was inevitable. My older brothers had left home, and I would soon be following them. It was several years since we had all been together at the "cottage" for our summer holidays and I knew we would never be there again as a family. So, I made a quick decision. I decided to have one last holiday alone at the place that meant more to me than anywhere else on earth. Although the presence of God fills the whole of creation, we tend to experience it more poignantly in those places and amongst those people whom we love most.

On the first day I did what I had been promising myself to do for many years. I climbed the mighty Ingleborough that towered over the surrounding countryside. I climbed it because, as Mallory said, "it is there," and for no other reason, but it turned out to be something of a spiritual experience that I did not expect.

Although it was a beautiful August day with only a few desultory clouds floating in the sky and scarcely affecting an all but perfect view of the Dales and the high moorlands, there was a gentle breeze that became stronger and stronger the higher I climbed. It was the first time I had ever climbed anything higher than Alderley Edge, the escarpment overlooking the Cheshire plain in the north of England where we used to go for our picnics as children, so I was fascinated by the views of the countryside I thought I knew so well.

If the experience of climbing was something of a revelation to me, it was nothing to what I experienced when I reached the summit. The strong breeze that had gathered momentum the higher I climbed suddenly exploded into a storm as I rose from the lee of the southern slopes to mount the summit. The sense of achievement that I had expected was tempered by the strange sense of fear that I felt as I stood there totally alone and wholly exposed to the elements that beset me from all sides and all but battered me to the ground. I understood for the first time why people of ancient religions believed that high places were holy places, places that were not only closer to the heavens where God had his abode, but places where his presence could be experienced embracing the body and seeping into the soul. The gentle caressing breeze that refreshed Adam "in the cool of the evening," and the devastating storms that often rage on mountain tops were one and the same manifestations of the breath of God's own mouth, his "Ruach," or his Spirit. This was his Holy Spirit at work in the world, formed from the primeval chaos at the dawn of time.

I remember reading a book some years ago called *The Idea of The Holy* by Rudolph Otto, in which the author characterized the human response to the experience of the Holy by the two words 'fear' and 'fascination'. The experience I had on Ingleborough helped me to understand what he meant, and to understand what the ancients felt, the sense of awe that they experienced, as Moses did on Sinai, when they approached their "holy places" on high. It has helped me to understand why so many people of every denomination, and none have felt drawn to climb mountains, not just because they are there, but because they sense someone else there, or at least they sense a presence there that they cannot feel elsewhere.

8 - Fear and fascination

St. Teresa of Avila used to try to prepare her sisters for the moment when their spiritual journey would lead them to the heights of Mount Carmel, because she knew from her own experience what, or rather whom, they would encounter as they approached the summit. The fascination of the One towards whom they were ascending would be instantly shattered by a frightening sense of fear, as he suddenly made his presence felt with a dramatic power and force that they had never experienced before.

The surprise and shock of the storm-force winds that surged around me at the summit were equaled by the magnificent views that took my breath away for a second time in a matter of moments. Besides the sense of fear that I felt, I was fascinated by the sense of presence too, that made me remain there for hours on end, soaking in the spiritual atmosphere that surrounded me, and gazing in awe at the magnificent views of the land where my ancestors had lived for generations before me. I wondered how many of them had been spiritually and physically refreshed at the very spot where I was now standing.

I could easily have spent the rest of my life climbing one mountain after another, like so many others who are lured onwards and upwards by the strange sense of fear and fascination that characterizes the ascent of a mountain, but another ambition took hold of me that day. I felt drawn to another ascent that had drawn so many of my spiritual forebears before me. I had no intention of entering Carmel, but I wanted to scale its heights, and I was ready and willing to go.

9

Converging streams

The climbing of the great Ingleborough set the scene for a week of solitude in our little cottage where I was led within myself as never before. It was the first time I ever reflected on my own inner life.

It seemed to have been composed of two parallel worlds, the world of religious experience and the world of mystical experience, that had developed side by side without ever meeting in any real way that enabled the one to make sense of the other. The world of religious experience was specifically Catholic, it was the world of Sunday Mass and weekly confession, of days of fasting and abstinence, of special feasts and holidays. It was the world of Catholic schools, of catechism to teach me my faith and to show me how to live it, of apologetics to show me how to reason round it and explain it to others, of annual retreats to set me alive in the Church with what bored me to death in the classroom.

The world of what I called my mystical experience was not specifically Catholic at all. It was an experience I had in common with others, other Christians of different traditions from my own, with Muslims and Jews, with Buddhists and Hindus, with Gnostics and agnostics and atheists too. They all seemed to have access to the same experience that I had at first thought was personal to me alone, although they all interpreted it according to their own religious or non-religious points of view. After all, why shouldn't everyone feel the touch of the One who loved them into being in the first place, and who loves them still no matter where or when they happen to be born, or what particular tradition they happen to be born into. Even dreary apologetics had taught me that God calls everyone to what everyone wants more than anything else.

As I reflected on my life, I thought it strange that I never experienced through the practice of my Catholic faith what I experienced on my beloved moors, through my favorite music, or on those mysterious nights when I would gaze for hours at the milky way and much more - experiences that made me mourn for days without knowing what had moved me. There had been occasional "feelings" that filled me with a certain peace of mind after "a good confession," or a sense of goodness as I walked home after early morning Mass, or was it merely smugness? My emotions had been moved from time to time too during parish missions, or at the singing of the Credo at Lourdes, or at the Easter blessing in St. Peter's Square, but never anything to compare with those profound and personal experiences that did not depend on the rites and rituals of the Church I was brought up in.

These two streams of experience seemed to have trickled through my life side by side without ever meeting, at least not in a way that I could understand. Then I was introduced to St Augustine at the beginning of the school retreat only two weeks after that unforgettable holiday.

Augustine had been a pagan when he experienced the Creator peering out at him through creation, and penetrating him with his presence, but it did not satisfy him, just as it had not satisfied me. It simply made his heart more and more restless, as it had made mine. But Augustine had a perceptive mind that enabled him to see so simply and so swiftly what lesser minds always seemed to complicate. If the Creator could make himself present through his work how much more could he make himself present through his Masterwork.

Suddenly I could see through Augustine's eyes that the One I had never fully encountered in either my religious or my mystical experience could be encountered in Christ, in whom and for whom everything was created from the beginning. In him my two separate streams would converge, my two separate worlds would become as one.

When the retreat master said that prayer was the only way to come to know him deeply and personally, I knew what I had to do. I joined the Monday meditation group, "Handley's half hour" as it was called. However, despite seeing what I ought to do with my mind, I needed something, or someone, to move my heart. I received the inspiration I needed from two of the teaching staff; one was a layman, the other a priest.

10

St Martin Buber

I don't think Mr Hogg would have been employed in the first place had his predecessor not suddenly dropped dead on his way to school. Mr Hogg was what was called in those days a "beatnik" and would not in the normal way of things have been accepted as a suitable candidate to teach English to the sixth form. He always wore a pair of filthy denim trousers, a multi-colored shirt, a grubby old duffel coat, and sandals, even when it was snowing. When he wasn't delivering brilliant lectures on English literature, he was to be found in the library reading existential philosophy. We idolized him.

I even took to reading Martin Buber, the man he continually quoted in class. He lent me his book *I and Thou*, which I wrestled with for weeks before throwing in the towel. I gave up trying to become an existential philosopher and decided to look like one instead, like the other boys in the class who fell under the spell of the remarkable Mr Hogg.

Unfortunately for all of us the board of governors failed to fall under the same spell and Mr Hogg was dismissed at the end of term. Several years later I came across a little book by Martin Buber in a second-hand bookshop; it was called *A Way of Life*. I read it from cover to cover on the bus home.

As an Orthodox Jew steeped in the rabbinical tradition, Martin Buber had chosen to detail the essence of his existential philosophy in stories, so that even I was able to understand what I was unable to understand before. One of his stories told of a carpenter from Lubin, who had a dream in which he saw a vast treasure of immense value that he was given to understand was meant for him if he could only find it. Immediately he gathered the tools of his trade together in an old carpetbag and set out in search of what he saw in that dream. After searching in vain through five continents for the treasure he believed he would find, he returned home tired and exhausted and flung his tools down on the ground beside the hearth he had left forty years before. The floorboards gave way under their weight to reveal the treasure he saw in that dream a generation earlier.

The Kingdom of God is within, and we search in vain if we search for his presence anywhere other than where we are now and in any other place than deep down within us. It is here that the One who is the "infinitely distant" has chosen to become the "infinitely near."

After God revealed himself to Moses in the burning bush, and gave him the law on Sinai, he told Moses to pitch another tent for he would now dwell among the people and travel with them. After they arrived at the promised land and the temple was built, the "Holy of Holies" at its center became the only place on earth where God's presence dwelt, behind a huge veil that separated it from the rest of the sanctuary.

When Jesus was finally glorified upon the cross, that veil was rent in two. The presence of God on earth was no longer to be found in the Holy of Holies in a man-made temple, but in the temple of Christ's own body and the bodies of every man and woman who freely choose to receive it. This is why Jesus himself said that the Kingdom of God is within you, as it was within him, and why St. Paul said that our very bodies are now the temples of the Holy Spirit.

Funnily enough it took a Jewish philosopher who rejected Jesus to help me realize one of the most profound truths that Jesus ever taught. I've stopped going on the pilgrimages that meant so much to me in the past; time is short so why should I waste any more time looking without for what I can only find within? I'm not trying to suggest that we shouldn't seek out special places to help us come closer to God, but they are special places only because they create the best possible environment for us to savor the One who has pitched his tent within us and who travels with us wherever we go.

I found such a place for myself ten years ago in a remote Benedictine monastery in Italy. The Abbot was an Englishman who explained to me how the vow of stability taken by the monks helped them to search for the presence within that so often eludes spiritual butterflies who find it difficult to settle anywhere for long. He didn't recognize me — why should he? But I recognized him. I couldn't see what he was wearing beneath his habit, but I wouldn't mind betting it was the same old denim trousers and the multicolored shirt. He was certainly wearing the same sandals.

When I asked him if he was called after St. Martin of Tours, he said no; he had called himself after another Martin whose memory was not celebrated in the Christian calendar.

11

A powerful magnetic force

I always found going to Mass a bore when I was a boy, so you can imagine how I felt when I had to go every day at boarding school. We had to be in chapel for morning prayer a quarter of an hour before Mass began, and then we had to stay there for ten minutes afterwards to make our thanksgiving. It was the longest ten minutes of the day until we found a way of filling it when one of the boys opened a 'book' on the 'side-altar stakes.'

I've never dared to admit it before, not even in confession, because the priest who took us for R.E. said that gambling was not necessarily a sin. We used to bet on how long it would take the priests who taught us, to say their private Masses, which they did during the Mass we attended at the high altar. Nobody ever beat "Pete the Pacemaker," so he had to carry a five-minute handicap or the 'bookie' would not take bets on him. Funnily enough nobody ever judged the quality of the priest by how long he spent at the altar. In fact, "Pete" was something of a hero for being able to read the Latin text faster than anyone else.

My attitude to the Mass took a dramatic turn for the better when I had to stand in for the sacristan for two weeks when he was sent home with chicken pox. I noticed that one of the priests, who was always in the chapel preparing for 'his Mass' long before we ar-

11 - A powerful magnetic force

rived, was still there making his thanksgiving not only when we left for breakfast, but after I returned to put the vestments away. One morning a message on the intercom meant I had to interrupt him. I do not want to sound pious, and I can assure you I was a million miles from piousness in those days, but it was like trying to intervene between some powerful magnetic force that held him in its grip. He had to drag himself away from something, or someone, who had his whole attention. It was the first time that I had encountered what I could only describe then as "holiness."

I'm not saying the priest was a saint, but somehow, I knew he was receiving the stuff that the saints are made of, and it had something to do with the Mass that until then had meant little if anything to me. I didn't tell any of the other boys what I had experienced because apart from anything else I could not put it into words, but I no longer took any further part in the "side-altar stakes."

Although that priest did not teach religion, except to the third form, there was something about him that set him apart. He was not 'one of the boys', nor did he ever seek cheap popularity, but he was held in greater respect than any of the other teachers. Sometimes during class, he would go into a sort of a trance and would just stare into space as if what usually determined the direction of his eyes was drawn elsewhere so that they were left 'on hold' to gaze intently at nothing in particular.

Only one boy ever took advantage of his strange moments of listlessness, and he ended up with a black eye, because the other boys somehow knew there was something special about that priest. They seemed to have realized that these moments of distance somehow made him closer to them through the kindness and compassion that seemed to radiate from him in such a gentle unobtrusive way. I felt privileged because I knew something that none of the other boys knew. I knew the secret source of this priest's inner strength, and I had, albeit briefly, experienced it for myself.

My experience not only changed my attitude to the Mass, but towards the priesthood too, though that is another story. What this story made me realize was that there was some awesome power in the Mass that I had never imagined before, a source of power that could be received only by those who were prepared to create the dispositions of mind and heart to receive it. I have experienced all sorts of liturgies over the years, from solemn High Masses to house Masses, from long charismatic Masses to short side-altar Masses, but the ones that have impressed me most have been those, of whatever genre, where the celebrant not only represented Christ but somehow embodied him by his openness to receive for himself what he was trying to communicate to others.

I am quite convinced that the renewal we all desire will be well under way when the priests we look to for leadership can lead us back to the Mass, with the personal prayerfulness that will enable them to receive for themselves what we want to receive from them more than anything else.

12

New horizons

I was acquainted with Anderson for years, though I had never really known him personally. I thought he was a bit of a 'wet' because he had no interest in sport and would avoid all games like the plague, so I avoided him. Why waste my time with a wimp? Then, to my horror I had to share a room with him on the school pilgrimage to Rome. If I stereotyped him as a boring immature swot it was quite clear that he had not stereotyped me by the easy, friendly way he behaved towards me.

He was so easy to talk to, and carried his obviously superior scholarship lightly, treating me as an equal though it was soon evident to me that I was not. He introduced me to the arts, to music and to the wide range of cultural interests and pursuits that had made him into a witty intelligent young person whom I could not help but respect and admire. I was grateful for his friendship and have been grateful to him over the years, for what he did for me by opening up artistic, literary and cultural horizons that may never otherwise have been open to me.

After I spent several months going to the Monday meditation group run by the school spiritual director, I had a sort of déjà vu experience that I realize had been triggered off by my newfound friendship with Anderson. I'd been acquainted with the person I was coming to know through meditation for years, but I never really knew him personally. I'd known the gospel story and its main teaching for as long as I could remember, without being able to recall who had taught it to me. I'd assimilated it by a sort of spiritual osmosis, as I grew up.

Of course, I knew about "Our Blessed Lord," as he was always called in those days, but I could not say I knew him personally. I believed in him, believed he was the Son of God, and turned to him often enough when I needed something, but there was never much of a personal relationship that developed beyond using him as a sort of panacea, a cure-all, find-all, do-all, whom I only turned to when it was to my advantage.

All that changed thanks to Father Handley and those Monday meditation meetings. If Anderson had opened up new horizons in my cultural life, the person I met through meditation opened up new horizons for my spiritual life. For the first time in my life Jesus Christ became a real living person to me. The more I tried to meditate on the gospels, the more I came to know him, admire him and even love him in a way I would never have dreamt possible before. Father Handley had encouraged us all to begin by turning to St. John's Gospel, reading it slowly and prayerfully and poring over its every word as one would pore over poetry to savor its meaning.

I began with the discourse at the Last Supper, then as the weeks went by I turned to the other famous discourses that were so rich and full of meaning that they moved me more than I would ever have thought possible. Then finally I began to meditate on the prologue that I had read often enough before without ever understanding it. What had meant nothing to me before suddenly meant everything to me and explained what had been quite inexplicable in the past. Jesus Christ was not just the most lovable person who had been born into this world of ours, but the person in whom the

12 - New horizons

world itself had been born at the beginning of time. In him everything came into being, and everything that was in him was permeated through and through with his presence. This presence can be experienced by those born into his world, who have been made in his image and likeness, as I had already discovered for myself.

The two streams of spiritual experience that had never met before now met in Christ. The mysterious presence of the person I'd encountered in brief mystical experiences in the countryside, by the sea, on clear moonlit nights, was one and the same person I'd met but never really known in my religious experience. The new insights that I received from St. John's Gospel drew together the two disparate streams in my spiritual experience that I was never able to reconcile before, making sense of my past and making me commit myself for the future to what has become the habit of a lifetime.

I formed two deep and lasting friendships in the sixth form. The first has taught me more and more about God's world, the second how that world has been mirrored in the world of man.

13

A spiritual lifeline

Despite the influences that I have already described, I did not turn to prayer because I was a particularly pious youth but because I was particularly needy and nobody I knew seemed to understand me, so I thought God might. It is all very well to decide to turn to God in prayer, but the question is, how do you do it?

Fortunately, even if nobody understood anything about dyslexia at the school I went to, at least someone knew something about turning to the only One who did. It is still the only school I've ever known that had a spiritual director, who, every Monday evening, gave a class on how to pray for all who chose to attend it. Father Handley spoke in such a quiet and gentle way that you felt compelled to listen to all he had to say, because you felt he was a practitioner himself in the practice you wanted to master. What I liked about his talks was that he did not just talk about prayer, he gave us practical examples of how to do it.

Of all the memory jogs to which he introduced us the one I found most useful was made up of the Latin word for Father, 'Pater'. In later years I added to it the Latin word Noster, 'Our' so that for the rest of my life the two words 'Pater Noster' have always provided me with a spiritual lifeline to help me turn to God when all else failed. I've explained elsewhere how I've used them at various stages of my life, but I am constantly finding that over the years I keep using them in different ways. The philosopher Hegel said, "As we get older, we return to the ways we prayed in our youth only to understand them more deeply than we did then." Let me explain, how I'm using them at present in the hope that they may be of some help to you.

I use 'Pater' to begin with to place myself in the Presence of God (P), then to prostrate myself inwardly in an act of Adoration (A) before the utterly Other, the transcendent majesty of the One who has chosen to make his home within us. The realization of what this means leads me to Thanksgiving (T) for what I have received and what I know I will continually receive to the end of time and beyond. The more I am able to realize just who God is and what he has done for me the more I become aware of how much I have failed to become what he wants of me. Then the Examination of conscience (E) that I try to make each day comes a little more easily. And so too does the act of Repentance (R) that follows it.

When I have finished using the first part of the memory jog, I move on to the second part, either immediately or at some later time in the day, depending on how long the first part takes to complete. The (N) reminds me to pray for the Needs of others, particularly those who have a right to expect my prayers and those I have promised to pray for. This ensures that no day passes without my remembering to pray for both the living and the dead. Then I pray for my own needs. After this I make what I was always taught to make as a boy the moment I awakened in the morning — my morning Offering (0). More's the pity that it seems to have gone out of fashion these days. When I've offered up the day ahead, I try to Surrender (S) myself totally to the will of God, as Jesus did throughout his life and most perfectly in his death. When this has been done there is nothing left but to Trust (T), and so I try to put my trust totally in the One I keep failing, but who I know will never fail me. Then I spend a few minutes trying to Examine (E), not my conscience this time, but the day ahead to prepare myself for everything in it that I can foresee and to ask God to help me particularly with what I cannot. Finally, I Resolve (R), with God's help, to make a better job of it than I did the day before. I always try to get rid of anything that is too formal or too contrived and to address God in my own words and in my own way.

I have never forgotten the words of St. Teresa of Avila that I first read during a school retreat. "There's only one way to perfection and that is to pray; if anyone points in another direction then they are deceiving you." As prayer is so important then, I'd like to spend some time examining in a little more detail each of the steps that I have just mentioned in turn (chapters 17-27). But first I would like to introduce you to a few preliminary reflections that may be of some help to you, as they have helped me over the years (chapters 14-16).

14

The empty tomb

It was almost twenty years ago that I was offered my first free holiday. It came like a bolt out of the blue. All I had to do was to meet a group of pilgrims from the Outer Hebrides, bundle them on to a plane at Luton airport, and deliver them in one piece to a Franciscan priest in Tel Aviv. It all sounded too good to be true, but it was true, and it turned out to be one of the most important spiritual experiences of my life.

It had all happened so quickly that I did not have time to think about it, and when I did, I'm ashamed to admit I thought of it as a free holiday rather than as a pilgrimage. Of course, I would visit the holy places and consider it a privilege, but my pilgrimages in Italy had stretched my credulity to breaking point. I had become hard-bitten and sceptical; only hard facts and incontestable evidence would impress me. I had no intention of wasting my time visiting dubious places where Jesus was supposed to have said this or done that, when I could be sunning myself by the Mediterranean.

But I was in for something of a surprise. Oh yes, there were plenty of contentious places and pious legends by the bucketful, but there were more hard facts than I had imagined, more than enough to keep me happy and off the beaches, to return home as white as I had come. It was the Holy Sepulchre that impressed me most. Not the architecture but the atmosphere of the place that touched me more deeply than I would have imagined.

Fr Kenneth, the friar who met us at the airport, lived and worked in the Holy Land for most of his life. He turned out to be a mine of information and seemed to have a key to every place that you really should see, and even to places that you should not! I do not know whether it was a case of heart over mind, but I believed implicitly in the historical evidence that he detailed. It seemed to prove beyond reasonable doubt the authenticity of the place where Christ was crucified and died, and the place where he was buried and rose from the dead.

On the night before we left, Fr Kenneth's famous key opened a door to me that seemed closed to everyone else, and opened to me an experience that has affected me deeply to this day. Although the doors to the Holy Sepulchre are closed every night and cannot be opened until the next morning no matter what, I was allowed to remain inside for the whole night, with a room to myself in the Franciscan friary within. I never went into that room. I spent all the time before the midnight office at Calvary and the time after it alone in the empty tomb. I was so overcome that I began to wish I could spend the rest of my life in that friary so that I could return again and again, night after night, to what must be the holiest place on earth, the place where Christ had lain and from which he rose from the dead.

Then suddenly, in a matter of moments, I had a spiritual experience that changed everything. I did not see anything, I did not hear anything, but the words of God spoke to me in a way they had never spoken to me before or since. In one sense it was nothing spectacular; but in another sense it irrevocably changed my whole attitude to the Resurrection that I believed in since I was a child, but which had never really touched me in the way it touched me that night.

14 - The empty tomb

I do not claim that the words came directly from God or anything like that; they most certainly came from my subconscious, but I'm sure God gave them a bit of a push. The words were these: "You are looking for Jesus of Nazareth who was crucified. See, here is the place where they laid him. He is risen now. He is not here. He has gone before you into Galilee." I changed instantly. I no longer wanted to live in that friary for the rest of my life, I did not even want to return to the tomb where Christ once lay in the past. The empty tomb suddenly lost its importance, though not its significance. The meaning of the Resurrection struck me acutely as never before, it was as if someone had said *ephphatha* and my eyes were opened to a truth that I had known with my head, but which had never fully penetrated my heart. Although my spiritual understanding had not substantially changed, it was totally transformed in a way that I find difficult to put into words. It was as if I had spent years looking at the Resurrection from the outside, as framed in a stained-glass window, then suddenly seen it again, this time from the inside with the sun shining through it.

The Resurrection meant that Jesus had been swept up out of the world of space and time in which he lived before, not to leave us but to be closer to us than ever before, as he promised "even to the end of time." Before the Resurrection he was limited by a physical body that could only be in one place at a time, so meeting him would have been as difficult as meeting any major personality in our time. But that has all changed now because the same otherworldly power that raised him out of this world on the first Easter day enabled him to re-enter it on every day. Sacred times and sacred places are only man-made reminders of the One who is present at every time and in every place to men and women of faith who choose to receive him.

Old fools live in the past, young fools live in the future. I know one fool who's lived in both, but thanks to Kenneth's famous key he is trying to live a little more fully in the present. It is the only place he knows to meet the Man he wants to meet more than anyone else in the world.

15

The present continuing tense

I remember visiting some Irish friends of mine, whose father was busy digging in the garden as I was leaving the house. When asked what he was doing, he replied, "I do be digging the garden." It had to be explained to me that this rather unusual expression was in fact a literal translation of what in Irish is called the present continuing tense. It means I have been digging the garden, I am digging the garden, and when you stop bothering me by asking the obvious, I will continue to dig the garden.

A few days later I was trying to explain to a class of eight-year-olds how Jesus had gone back to heaven at Easter to live with his Father, when the smallest boy in the class said, "But what does he do all day?" Without thinking, I replied, "He do be loving every one of us all day long." In other words, he has been loving us, he is loving us, and he will continue to love us to the end of time and beyond. This is exactly what St John meant when he said that God is love.

Although St John's Gospel was written in Greek, St John himself was not a Greek intellectual who would distinguish precisely between what a person is and what they do; he was an existential Jew. To him what a person did was far more important than what they were, though in fact the two are not easily separable. A person is what they do. God is love because he is loving all the time, as is the Son he sent to enable us to do likewise.

The Mr. Men series of books were in vogue at the time so I was able to say to the children that Jesus is "Mr. Loving," because that is what he does all day. It was a title that meant much to me, because it was the one I used myself many years before when I was first introduced to "Mr. Loving." Thanks to the Irish present continuing tense I was able to understand and explain to the children the most important truth of our faith. I do not know enough Hebrew to be able to say whether or not it has a present continuing tense, but Jews are certainly more concerned with what God does than in trying to define what he is.

If God is loving us all the time then the most important thing we can do is to open ourselves out to receive that love, and to do it all the time. If someone loves us and we want to receive their love, then the best thing we can do is to love them in return.

It's exactly the same in our relationship with God. Our love for him is like a lightning conductor that attracts and then directs his love so that it is shafted deep down to set our human being afire with the divine. That is why the first of the commandments is to love God with your whole heart and mind and with your whole being. Then the second commandment follows as a matter of course. No one who is full of love can help but overflow with what they have received so that others can share in the goodness that it generates.

That is why everyone loves a wedding because the love that the couple has for each other is somehow infectious and nobody can come close to love without being touched by what they themselves want more than anything else. That is why marriage is a sacrament — not just for the bride and groom but for all those who have come to witness their love, because they not only see God's love embodied in the couple's love for each other, but they receive something of that love themselves to the measure that they are open to receive it. Only those who are spiritually dead can leave a wedding without a smile on their face through experiencing once again something of what makes life worth living.

This is all very well, it's very wonderful too, but we cannot spend our lives running from one wedding to another to experience something of the divine that is embodied in the human, nor do we need to. The divine love is primarily embodied in the physical but glorified body of Jesus, "Mr. Loving," who is loving us at every moment so that we can be constantly open to receive what he is endlessly giving, no matter where we are, no matter what we are doing. Although the most important truth in the spiritual life is that God is loving us all the time, this truth will do nothing to change us until we begin to take practical steps to receive it. God never stops loving us, but we may stop loving him. And when we do, his love is totally ineffective, not in itself but in ourselves, because it can only transform those who choose to receive it.

The secret of the spiritual life, then, is learning how to allow the love that surrounds us at all times to enter into us and to do for our weak human nature what was done for the weak human nature that Jesus freely chose to enter. This is the way he chose to show us how to receive what transformed him into the person my class came to call "Mr. Loving".

16

Drop out, turn on, tune in

Most people would not think of Usain Bolt as a mystic, but he certainly seems able to put himself into a deep mystical trance almost at will. I noticed him for years as he prepared for the hundred metres. Then I noticed how other athletes and other great performers are able to do the same. Take the snooker player, Stephen Hendry, for instance. He may be surrounded by thousands of people at the world snooker championships, but he might as well be on a desert island for all the difference it makes. He enters his own world where nothing else seems to matter but the game in hand.

Watch Fred Couples on the golf course. See him preparing to make a vital putt, lost to everything and everyone in the world that can distract him from his purpose. But notice how, if something happens to break into his concentration, he begins once again to go through all the rituals that enable him to draw back into the strange trance-like state that produces the single-minded concentration without which he'd never succeed.

I was delighted to see many of the athletes and sports personalities I've admired over the years taking part in a television documentary and to hear them speaking about the rituals they use to draw them into the trance-like concentration that enables them to reach their full potential. I found the program not only fascinating but extremely practical. Now I'm not suggesting it inspired me to "go for gold" or enter the "Open," but it did enable me to learn from them something that could help me in my spiritual life.

How much easier prayer would be, for instance, if I could only learn how to cut myself off from the day-to-day world as these athletes do and enter into the trance-like state that would enable me to concentrate, for a time at least, on the "one thing necessary" for my spiritual life to flourish. I think what impressed me most was that, apart from their particular expertise and their ability to "drop out, turn on and tune in" almost at will, these were just ordinary people like me, living otherwise commonplace, uneventful lives. They did not spend the rest of their time living in deserts or caves or hermitages. They had developed a method of almost instant mental detachment that could be of immense benefit to the rest of us who, like them, live in the same busy world from which we need to escape for periods of time to "rest awhile" and draw strength from the only One who can help us.

What I found most interesting was that all of them had different rituals that led them into the trance-like stillness that they all agreed was essential. For some it was a solitary walk, for others listening to their favorite music or just sitting alone with "a nice cup of tea" while they drew their thoughts together. Others were far more systematic. They used different methods of deep rhythmical breathing, with or without the use of words that some had adapted for their own use. They rubbished the idea that they were in fact praying, insisting that their methods were used simply to draw them into a gentle trance like state that would enable them to concentrate on what was the 'one thing necessary' at that particular moment of their lives. The fact of the matter is that we are unable to flee to the desert like some of our spiritual forebears, but we can learn from these athletes how to drop out of the world we live in for a time, to turn on and tune in to another world that can alone replenish and refill us with what we need most. I would like to go to one of our local churches, but most of them are locked up all day, so I settle down in my old recliner with a "nice cup of tea." Then I try to empty my mind as best I can and to drop out as I listen to a piece of my favorite music. This helps me to turn on and tune in to the presence of God when the music ends, and leads me into a still, contemplative silence.

One thing is certain: everyone must find their own way to relax and to discover the rituals that help them best to be still if they would learn to concentrate like those athletes. Then they will be able to focus so much better on "the one thing necessary" and the one person necessary, "Mr. Loving" who can alone satisfy their deepest needs and most profound aspirations.

17

Spirituality from the "kitsch 'n sink"

I wish Sr. Wendy Beckett would consider running one of those correspondence courses for artistic ignoramuses like me. It would at least spare my friends and acquaintances the embarrassment of hearing me parrot, "Well, I don't know much about art, but at least I know what I like."

I know what I do not like too, and I do not like that hideous holy picture in my aunt's house that takes pride of place in her kitchen. It depicts Jesus as an effeminate blue-eyed blond, suspended in outer space, dressed in pastel shades of blue, green and gold, with rays of light shafting from his heart. My aunt did try to explain to me that it was an "artist's impression" of a vision experienced by some South American mystic, but I quickly changed the subject to her inimitable apple pies and the one she promised to make me for my birthday.

I would not even have given her kitsch masterpiece a second thought had it not come back to haunt me over the years. You see the thing is, it does have some merit — not artistic but symbolic merit. It does symbolize better than any picture I know how God is present to us at all times in Jesus. Depicting him in some strange vacuous world in outer space somehow manages to express the supra-temporal, supra-spatial dimension of the world he entered into on the first Easter day. The radiance that surrounds him symbolizes the fullness of life that filled him, and the rays that beam outwards represent that same life radiating on to and into all who would receive it. Precisely because he was raised out of the world of space and time, he is able to enter into it more deeply and more effectively in every place and at every time simultaneously, as he promised, "to the consummation of the world." While he remained on earth, he was necessarily restricted. Only a few people at a time could meet him, listen to him, and receive from him what is now open to everyone.

The artistic interpreters of St. Margaret Mary's visions of the Sacred Heart did for an older generation what my aunt's South American mystic and his artistic interpreter is attempting to do for this. They are both trying to give a powerful symbolic representation of the most important truth of our faith, namely that God is present to us now in Jesus, who has been raised to live forever by a love that is endlessly poured out so that we can choose to receive it.

When I was a young boy, I used to think that God's presence meant that he was following us all the time to spy on everything we did, so I used to turn round as fast as I could to see if I could catch him at it. When I was told he was not so much following us around but rather looking down on us, not to catch us out but to watch over us, I gave up what was beginning to turn into a compulsive habit. But it was only after years of studying what was then called the new theology that I came to a different idea of the presence of God that was far more dynamic. It was the idea of his presence in Jesus risen and glorified, that was bursting with the uncreated life and energy that is love, that shafted outwards like a radioactive isotope. Unfortunately, I didn't know what a radioactive isotope looked like, and anyway an inanimate symbol could never have conveyed to me the new and exciting idea that I had of the all-giving, all-penetrating presence that was at all times radiating outwards to transform us.

17 - Spirituality from the "kitsch 'n sink"

It was from then onwards that whenever I began my prayer by trying to put myself in the presence of God, my aunt's "masterpiece" began to frame itself in my imagination. I know it's kitsch, I can't help that, but it's the only picture I know that helps me to prepare for prayer by visualizing the presence of God and how his transforming love reaches out to us through Jesus. It not only helps me to visualize it, but it also helps me to realize it too, and to genuinely receive it. After all that is what prayer is ultimately all about.

Dear Sr. Wendy Beckett, I know it is only pride and pseudo-sophistication that makes me ask, but could you please recommend a more acceptable masterpiece to frame in my imagination? It must do for me what my aunt's "masterpiece" does, but with a little more artistic credibility. If it's acceptable to you, I know it will be acceptable to me. Thanks.

18

Familiarity breeds conceit

Beau Brummell and the Prince Regent were almost inseparable, until the famous socialite began to take their friendship for granted and forgot who his friend was. He became overfamiliar and his familiarity bred all but contempt. An inevitable rift took place that became final after Brummell's impertinent remark to a friend of his, who was accompanying the Prince on his morning stroll. Cutting the Prince dead, he said, "Who's your fat friend?" Now it was the Prince Regent's turn to cut Brummell dead, and it was a long and humiliating death, as a social outcast, debtor, and pauper, who finally died in an asylum in Caen in 1840.

It is all too easy to take friendship for granted and forget the respect that is due to the friend, especially when that friend is morally or socially one's superior. The first disciples never took advantage of the friendship that Jesus offered them because the power of his personality made that impossible.

The Prince Regent had all, if not more, of the faults of Beau Brummell so his weak personality almost invited the lack of respect that preceded the ultimate ridicule. The disciples of Jesus, however, saw no weakness in the man who loved them and insisted on calling them his friends; indeed, they came to see that he was also the human embodiment of the One who made them. After the Resurrec-

18 - Familiarity breeds conceit

tion, all who came to hear of what God had done in Jesus and of the friendship he offered them rarely took that friendship for granted, let alone knowingly overstepped the mark. But several generations later, after all who had known him personally were dead, more and more Christians began to misinterpret the friendship into which baptism had introduced them. It was a gradual process that was to begin without malice. It was just that Jesus seemed so close to them, so near at hand, that they began to treat him not so much as an equal but as an older brother.

Now, as the emphasis on Jesus' human nature began to loom larger and larger, the emphasis on his divine nature began to recede, so when a priest called Arius denied that Jesus was God many came to accept his heresy. If friendship with Jesus had not led to contempt, it had led to perhaps the most serious misunderstanding about him in the Church's history. At the time, the majority of the faithful fell into Arianism, and the effect of the heresy was so great that it has influenced Christian theology and spirituality down to the present day. "Christ is God" was the slogan that was repeated again and again by the Church as she tried to stamp out the heresy that threatened to destroy her. As a result, in subsequent centuries it was the divinity of Christ that was emphasized, often at the expense of his humanity.

It is so difficult for those of us who have not known Jesus personally as the first disciples did to understand in a clear and balanced way that Jesus is both divine and human. He is not a superman or a demi-god, but truly Man and truly God at one and the same time. Whenever one nature is emphasized, it is usually at the expense of the other and an imbalance seeps by stealth into authentic Christian theology, liturgy, spirituality, and devotion. The truth is that the One who has chosen to enter into our world, and who chooses to be our personal friend, is also the All-Holy God by whom the world was created in the beginning. That is why in any authentic

Christian spirituality there must be a time for adoration, to "bend the knee" at the name of Jesus, to give him the honor and reverence that is due, and to give true balance to the friendship to which he has called us.

Beau Brummell lost the friendship that he desired more than any other because he forgot that his friend was also the Prince and the future King. Whenever we forget to pay due honor and reverence to the One who's chosen to call us and make us his friends then that friendship is doomed. If Christian tradition teaches us to begin prayer by reminding us of how God is continually present to us, in and through the abiding presence of Jesus, then it teaches too that we should never end it before we have humbly prostrated ourselves before him, else we forget ourselves and the adoration that we owe him.

19

Thank God for being God

Instead of Christmas crackers the Knights of St. Columba bought "Christian crackers" for the parish party. So instead of wearing paper hats everyone wore paper haloes, and received miniature plastic saints, and instead of side-splitting jokes they could meditate on mind-bending religious epigrams. Mine not only bent my mind but tied it in knots for weeks trying to work out what it meant.

It was ascribed to a certain H. Smith (circa 1630) and went something like this: "He is not thankful before God who only thanks him for his benefits." I don't think I ever fully unravelled its meaning until I went to a retreat given by Archbishop Anthony Bloom three weeks later. At the end of the retreat the Sister in charge said, "I not only want to thank you for what you have given us, but to thank you for being you." It was a popular religious cliché at the time that usually made me squirm, especially when the said Sister not only thanked me for unblocking the convent drains the day before but added the "thank you for being you" bit at the end of it. However, when applied to Archbishop Anthony Bloom it certainly made sense; not only that but it gave sense to the religious epigram that had been tying my mind in knots ever since the parish party.

The Archbishop gave us a lot to think about in his talks, but he gave us far more by just being what he was, a remarkable embodiment of the Man in whose name he preached. It was silly to thank me for being me just because I unblocked the drains, but it wasn't silly to thank him for being him because what he was had far more importance than what he said, though he said more to move me than any other preacher before or since.

Now I could see what Mr H or Ms H Smith meant. If we only thank God for what we manage to get out of him then we have hardly begun to thank him as we should. He should be thanked for being God, for being justice, for being goodness and beauty, and for displaying his inner glory in the glory of creation that surrounds us, and for the Masterpiece of creation, whom he has sent to inhabit us.

When I was a small boy, I went to see Aladdin at The Hippodrome in London where Buttons introduced us to the two magic words that would open any door, "please" and "thank you." It was not enough to say, "Open Sesame" to enter Aladdin's cave unless you added "please," and if you forgot to say the words "thank you" the door would close before you could enter it. It was the same with the genie of the lamp who would give you nothing until you had said "please," and would take it away again if you forgot to say, "thank you." From then on I never forgot to use my magic words, most especially in prayer when I used them to get what I wanted out of God. I never forgot to thank him for what he gave me for fear he would take it away. But my prayer of thanksgiving never led me far beyond myself, beyond my own needs and my own little world.

When I began to thank God for being God, however, it was as if I was raised up beyond myself and into God's world, if only for a brief moment, where my prayer life reached higher peaks than ever before. If you don't know what I mean, try this little experiment and you soon will. When you've thanked God for what he's done for you start thanking him for what he does for everyone just by being what he is. Turn to the Gloria of the Mass. Recite it slowly and prayerfully, making every word your own and you'll find you are taken out of yourself into God's world where you praise him, thank him, and give him glory with all those who learned to thank God for being God. Recite the canticle of Daniel that is recited by "the Church at prayer" on Sunday mornings and you'll find yourself thanking and giving praise and glory to God with the whole of creation. What is more you will also find that the further you enter into this world the more you will forget yourself and the world where you only thanked him for what he gave you and you will come alive if only for a time, in the world where you want to be for all time.

Thanking God for being God leads into the heights of prayer where praise, glory and thanksgiving become as one, and we become more at one with God and with ourselves than ever before.

20

Power in weakness

There is always some wiseacre on the interview panel who suddenly says, "And what do you think your biggest weaknesses are, Mr Torkington?"" He usually chooses the moment when your confidence is at its height and you've been presenting yourself as Mr Total Competence, who could do the job in his sleep. Suddenly you have to backpedal warily, losing as little composure as possible, while showing that even you are human after all, with faults and failings like the rest of humankind.

Skilful operators can usually turn the situation to their advantage by humbly admitting to faults that just happen to make them an even more desirable candidate. You know the sort of thing I mean: "I'm afraid I have a punctuality problem — I simply can't be late for an appointment," or "I do tend to neglect my family sometimes, because I can't bring myself to leave the office until I've cleared my desk." Anyway, the point I'm trying to make is that although these "smart alecks" can be a bit of a pain in the neck, and it's a real joy to get the better of them, they are right to try to find out whether or not their interviewees are aware of their faults and failings.

In the only retreat I remember from my school days, the well-known Jesuit Fr. Bassett said, "If your friends won't tell you your faults pay an enemy to do it for you." The central scriptural theme that runs

20 - Power in weakness

through the Old and New Testaments is, in the words of St. Paul, "God's power finds full scope in human weakness." So, if there are those who are totally oblivious of their weakness, they will not turn to the only One who can help them.

A famous Dominican preacher used to like shocking congregations into listening to him by shouting at the top of his voice, "Your sins will save you." But before they could burn him at the stake, he explained that St. John insisted that we are calling God a liar if we say we are not sinners. That is what we are, that is where we begin, and that is where we stay unless we learn, like the saints, to turn our greatest weakness into our greatest strength. The secret that leads to sanctity begins with that moment of truth when we begin to realize what sinners we are and experience the need to turn to the only One who can make us into the Christlike persons we want to be.

That is why from the earliest times the practice of examining one's conscience regularly grew, first amongst the Desert Fathers and then amongst those who were later influenced by the Fathers' profound spirituality. It was Fr Bassett who first taught me the importance of daily examination of conscience when I went to him for confession. I was in the full flush of my first fervour when I knelt before him to admit, as humbly as I could, that I could not exactly remember any sins since my last confession, but I nevertheless sought his blessing and spiritual advice. After a long pause he said, "Well, for your penance say three 'Hail Marys' in honor of your immaculate conception!"

Then he explained that it was only lack of insight that led me to believe I was wearing the confessor's crown — a crown that would be mine only in heaven if I ever made it. The first step to making it, he suggested, was to gain insight into the many faults and failings that I could not see because I had unfortunately been blinded, as so many are, by the sweet vapours of first fervour. Although he employed humour and irony to awaken me to the self-righteousness and pride that I had been totally unaware of, he did it with such kindness that I began to practice what I have since always tried to maintain with varying success over the years.

In recent times all too many priests and religious have been deceived into believing that they can speed up the journey to self-knowledge by using questionable methods of analysis culled from the latest fashionable brands of pop-psychology that happen to be in vogue. So many of these methods can not only be dangerous to the dabblers themselves but can cause incalculable damage to those who fall under their powerful influence.

In the authentic Christian tradition, the examination of conscience takes place in the context of prayer and under the influence of the perfect psychiatrist, the "Holy Spirit," who is both truth and love at one and the same time. As he progressively makes us aware of our faults and failings, and of the deeper obstacles that prevent growth, he continually supports us with the love that enables us to become our true selves. This love becomes ever more penetrative and effective as the ever-deepening awareness of our weaknesses leads us to turn and open ourselves through daily prayer to the "power" who works in weakness. Then he can begin the process of making us into new and unique embodiments of the Man we have chosen to follow.

21

Actions speak louder than words

If morals maketh the man and manners maketh the gentleman, then Carruthers was the finest gentleman I ever met. Or so I thought for the first few weeks when we shared a flat together. However, as the weeks went by, I began to see that his manners were no more than a thin coat of veneer that hid the chipboard man within.

Casual visitors were as impressed with him as I was to begin with. He was always "so terribly sorry" for everything. He was "so terribly sorry" for beating you to the bathroom, "so terribly sorry" for keeping you waiting for half an hour, "so terribly sorry" for failing to clean the bath when he finished. He was "so terribly sorry" for emptying the fridge when he had his friends around, "so terribly sorry" for leaving the washing-up for you the following morning, "so terribly sorry" too for leaving my car with an empty tank when he borrowed it without asking. The trouble is, he was not sorry at all, and he kept on behaving in the same old way no matter what.

It is one thing to say you are sorry. It is quite another to mean it. If you mean it you do something about it. Next time round you clean the bath, you wash up your own pots, you remember to put petrol in the tank. All this happened many years ago when it was the custom to go to confession almost every week, so it made me think I was not much better myself. I mean I was always saying I was "so terribly sorry" after I made my confession, but I was always back the next week with the same little list.

Who could blame God for getting as fed up with me as I was with Carruthers? I think what really bugged me was that Carruthers' attitude made it quite clear that he had no respect for me at all, because everything he failed to do for me was done for any visitor he really liked or looked up to as his social superior. It was this that made me realize that if I loved and respected God a bit more my little list may get shorter with each passing week and the "number of times" may become fewer.

These thoughts made me turn back to the prayer that had once been so important to me and to the One from whom alone I knew I could receive the help and strength to become more the man he really wanted me to be. The truth of the matter is, it is all too easy to say, "so terribly sorry," so easy to rattle through an act of contrition without really meaning what we say. If we are genuinely sorry, we not only say we are sorry, but we try to do something about it, and that means turning to the only One who can help us.

That is why Jesus continually used the word "repent" when he called on people to change their lives. You see, this word means so much more than any other I've ever heard to describe what we sinners should do, if we really want to change our lives. The word Jesus used came from the Hebrew word "shub," which means "to return." To return home is how it is often used in the Old Testament; to return to one's father is how Isaiah used it. This is how Jesus used it when he proclaimed the good and exciting news that we have not only a God who is the Father who created us, but a "loving Dad" (Abba), who is continually communicating his life to us. Our lives will be changed radically and permanently for the better only if we freely choose to return and open ourselves to receive the love that is

21 - Actions speak louder than words

always there to forgive us, and to give us the strength to start again no matter how many times we fall.

I have just finished reading Henri Nouwen's book *The Prodigal Son*, in which he describes how Rembrandt's masterpiece helped him to understand the parable in a deeper way than ever before. If you want to know a little more about the meaning of repentance, it's a must. We can make an act of contrition and we should do so regularly, but that act of contrition only becomes really effective if we make it into an act of repentance too. In other words, it's not enough to say, like Carruthers, that we are "so terribly sorry". We need to do something about it.

We need to do more than make a firm purpose of amendment too. We need to turn back to the Father who wants to be a loving Dad, so that we can receive and experience the only love that will make us new. Only he can make us into the new men and women who are not only sorry for what we were, but serious travellers on the way to becoming what he wants to make of us.

22

Into another dimension

St Padre Pio was praying at his bedside when one of the community members burst into his room by accident. "Terribly sorry to interrupt your prayer," the brother said. "Not at all," said Padre Pio, "I was just praying for a happy death for my father." "But your father died ten years ago." "Yes, that's right," said Padre Pio.

Most of our actions are limited by the world of space and time in which we live, but prayer is not because it takes us into another dimension where the laws of space and time no longer apply. That other dimension is Christ, who is not only the alpha and the omega, the beginning and the end of all space and time, but present to every moment of it simultaneously. When prayer raises us up out of our world and into his it enables us to reach out to all who are in him, to all he can reach out to, whether they live in the past, the present or the future.

Some years ago, I went to The Royal Opera House in Covent Garden to the premiere of a new opera called Thérèse by John Tavener, based on St Thérèse of Lisieux. I had my misgivings. How could anyone manage to convey anything of the inner life of this unique saint in a theatrical performance, no matter how imaginative or inventive the production? I was wrong. Whether the opera will remain in the operatic canon as a musical masterpiece I have no idea, but it will certainly remain in my mind as a spiritual masterpiece.

The composer went to the heart of the prayer that united St Thérèse with Christ and enabled her to reach out to others through him. Though she lay dying in her simple bed that was placed center stage, he showed in a series of theatrical and musical master strokes how her prayer was effective for those for whom she prayed in the past, in the present and in the future. He showed how through her union with Christ the barriers of space and time were cast aside and how she was able to reach out to all for whom she prayed in, with, and through him.

Her room had only three walls, the fourth was open to the audience. It reminded me of the Eastern tradition that taught those who were called to the eremitical life that they must remember that their hermitages have only three walls. The fourth must be open to the world to which they must reach out through their solitary prayer. They may be in solitude but through prayer they are raised up and into the communion of saints, into union with all who are united together in Christ. That is why there is no such thing as private prayer in the Christian tradition, even though the pray-er may be totally alone in their own home, in the local church, on their death bed or in the furthest reaches of the most distant desert. They are present with all those who are living and loving in the family of Christ, and present to all those for whom they pray in their need. This is why the sincere prayer of the least of us is powerful far beyond our own personal spiritual resources alone.

All my immediate family are dead now, but I try to remember them each day and to pray for them as St Padre Pio prayed for his father. I try to pray for others too who have asked me to pray for them and whom I might otherwise forget despite the promise I made at the time. There's a wider world also that needs our prayers but rarely asks for them. An uncle of mine used his daily newspaper as a prayer book. He noted down those whose sufferings made him feel helpless and remembered them at the time he set aside for daily prayer. Just as you cannot give charity to every cause, you cannot pray for every cause by name either, so it's often a good idea to adopt one or two causes that have a special meaning for you.

Long before I could read, I picked up a book by chance and in it saw a picture of a man being cruelly tortured that haunted me for years and has left me to this day with a horror of torture and a deep concern for those who are tortured for whatever reason. This is the cause that I have always tried to adopt when I finish praying for those for whom I have a special responsibility. Although praying for others may seem to be the poor cousin of other spiritual exercises that appear more attractive, it's certainly not the case. If it is in giving that we receive then it is in reaching out to others in prayer that the selflessness of that act opens us, without our realizing it, to the only love that can satisfy our own needs more than anything else.

23

The only magic that matters

I was crazy about conjuring when I was a boy. It was my way of easing myself out of the fairy-tale world of mystery and make-believe and into the world of reality, otherwise known as school. I never quite lost my interest in magic, nor am I the only one if the television ratings are to be believed. Almost every magic show that's ever been screened has made it into the top ten. It is not just that magicians amuse, entertain, or baffle us; it's because they appeal to something deep down within us, something even deeper than the fairy-tale world we escaped into as children. They appeal to the pagan in us that wants to gain power over the world around us and the people in it, but most of all to gain power over God and make him act according to our will and not his.

That is why the ancient pagan world was awash with wizards and witches, magicians and magi, priests, and priestesses, all offering magical rites and rituals that promised to satisfy a person's every need. Even the chosen people finally fell prey to the magic rites of their neighbors which so sullied their sacrifices that God no longer wanted to accept them. The only sacrifice he really wanted of them was that of a pure and humble heart offered through everything they did. This was the offering that Jesus made with every fibre of his being throughout his life on earth. It is the same offering that he asked of all who would follow him, that they would love God with their whole hearts and minds and with their whole being. The way he lived his life was a practical example of how this could be done and the Spirit that enabled him to do it is the same Spirit that he continues to send to enable us to do likewise.

In ancient times people thought that magic could solve all their problems, even their biggest problem of all — the death that threatened them with oblivion. If only they could gain power over their gods, they would be saved from death to live on forever beyond the starry skies. When Jesus came it was to announce a new world order that put an end to magic. In this new world people could only be saved from all that threatened to diminish or destroy them by a love powerful enough to overcome even death.

The gospel tells the story of how this love progressively penetrated the life of Jesus, making his self-offering the most perfect that the world had ever seen. It promised this same love to all who chose to receive it, so that they could join with him in making the only offering that God really wants. This meant that in the future everyone could be a priest because no one else can offer for you what only you can give. That is why the first Christians knew no other priesthood than the priesthood of Christ and that of all Christians who chose to share in it. They exercised this priesthood at the weekly Eucharist where they received the help and strength to enable them to make their self-offering again and again through the most mundane tasks that made up their everyday lives.

In those early days there was no daily Mass, nor did such a practice emerge for many centuries to come. Gradually, however, a practice grew up that enabled the faithful to remind themselves continually of their priesthood and of their daily offering in, with and through Jesus. It was called the morning offering and many of us were taught to make it as children, but sadly it is no longer the widespread practice that it used to be.

23 - The only magic that matters

A short time ago I called on my plumber to borrow a spanner. When he opened his toolbox, I read the words "All for the glory of God" written under its lid. When I asked him about it, he said it helped to remind him of his morning offering throughout the rest of the day. I didn't even know he was a Christian. I only knew him as a good workman who'd never let you down and never overcharged you. Regrettably I had long since forgotten to say my morning offering: I was too busy studying the documents of the Vatican Council and lecturing others on the priesthood of the laity.

But thanks to my leaky radiator and my plumber's transparent goodness I returned once more to do what my mother taught me all those years before. For the first time in years, I became more consciously aware of the only priesthood that can change the dross of daily drudgery into gold. That is real magic, the sort that only love can perform. It's the only magic that matters to me now.

24

The whole truth and nothing but the truth

It made my hair stand on end to read such a thing in a Catholic weekly, particularly as the quotation had been specifically highlighted by the editor. It simply said, "We will not be asked to account for those actions that are performed under holy obedience."

If it had been printed in the Gestapo Gazette you could have understood it, but the Catholic Gazette? It represented the sort of mentality once common in religious life when young and gullible novices were told that they should leave their wills at the door on the way in, do everything without question, and look for inspiration to specially selected "saints" who were presented to them as having done likewise.

There is only one person who can demand that we unconditionally surrender our wills to his and that's not the prime minister or the president, nor any human potentate for that matter, not even the Pope. Papal infallibility is a very important but limited gift of the Holy Spirit, to help successive generations of Christians retain with certainty the essential teachings of Christ. Then they can the better surrender themselves unconditionally to the only One who has a right to demand such a total and complete offering of themselves. And what does God do when a person unconditionally surrenders themselves to him? In the words of my late professor of moral philosophy, he says, "You choose." God's will is that we choose. He is not a totalitarian tyrant who wants only our blind unquestioning obedience. He didn't create us with a mind to reason with and a will to choose with only to command us to deny and disregard what is his greatest gift.

The very first time Jesus opened his mouth in the gospels was to explain to his mother that he had come to do his Father's will, and his last words were to surrender himself to his father unconditionally. Throughout his life he made it clear that his "meat and drink" was to do his father's will in all things. This did not mean that he was a blind, unthinking automaton. If he had been he could not have done for us what only a free human being could have done.

His obedience to God meant that he used his will more, not less, that he made decisions, often terrifying and difficult decisions, like those he had to make while fasting in the desert, praying in Gethsemane, or dying on the cross, when the temptations that had taunted him throughout his life taunted him most of all. The very reason why he died on the cross was because he used his mind to distinguish between the authentic religious traditions of his forebears that he had come to complete and the cant and hypocrisy of his contemporaries, who had distorted it. It was his razor-sharp mind that enabled him to see how they had perverted the people in order to retain their own petty power and position and to enhance their own honor and glory rather than God's.

When others might have kept their mouths shut to save their skins, he spoke out openly because he had come to bear witness to the truth no matter what the cost, and the cost was very high. He did all this and suffered for it precisely because he freely chose to surrender himself unconditionally to his Father. When we freely choose to surrender ourselves to God it means that we must do what Jesus did, use our minds more, not less, to discover his truth, in the authentic tradition to which we belong, and to distinguish it from the cant and hypocrisy that always tries to distort it for personal gain and pre-ferment. Then, like Jesus, we must freely choose to bear witness to that truth, whether it is welcome or unwelcome, and at whatever cost. To surrender oneself to the truth means to seek out the truth actively through serious study and deep personal contemplation, so that we can distinguish between what is the inspired word of God and what is of man, what is living tradition and what is dead traditionalism, what is infallible and what is fallible. Then we must surrender ourselves to that truth with our whole mind and heart and with our whole being, and pro-claim it from the rooftops at no matter what personal cost, as Christ did before us.

This commitment to the truth that the gospel demands of all of us is uniquely embodied in the charism of the Dominican tradition, whose motto is Veritas. Some of them, like St Thomas, have excelled at defining it; others, like St Catherine of Siena and St Vincent Ferrer, at proclaiming it; and others, like Savonarola, at suffering for it. We can all learn from the great Dominican tradition what it means to surrender ourselves unconditionally to God, and to his truth. And in this way, we can embody the truth in all we do and all we say so that Christ can speak again to the contemporary world through us.

25

The Feel-Good Factor

He was given a job by a merchant bank when he came down from Oxford and promised a job for life, but after the takeover bid, he was made redundant. Fortunately, he secured a job as a computer programmer for a firm in the Thames valley that promised him the earth until they went bust a year later. Then he was given a high-powered job with one of the cross-channel ferry companies, till they started to lay men off thanks to the Chunnel. It was then he fell a prey to depression for several months, and who could blame him? He said the trouble was he felt he couldn't trust anyone anymore. He had been offered several other jobs but only on short-term contracts that made him fear the inevitable, and so he turned them down. For the first time in years, he felt secure, he said, because he had organized his own job for himself.

He thanked me for the coffee and carried on cleaning my windows, as he did everyone else's in Spennithorne Drive. I could sympathize with him because I had similar experiences myself, putting my trust in people whom I thought I could believe in, only to discover how gullible I was when they pushed me out of the job, I thought I would have for life. The worst thing of all, and this we both experienced, was that the life-long friends, whom we thought we could really trust, suddenly disappeared with the status we lost. It's no wonder the "feel-good factor" has vanished along with the yuppies in the eighties; nor will it return until people find they can trust once more.

Now I do not want to use this story to churn out pious platitudes about the spiritual life, like "If we only trust in God then everything will be all right," because it would not necessarily change our predicament at all. Our brave new world, that knows the price of everything and the value of nothing, cannot change just because we suddenly begin to trust in God, but we may! It's good to know that there is at least one rock to cling to in the shifting sands that surround us. If our material insecurity makes us trust in that rock, then the ill wind will certainly have blown some good. If we've done all we can and all we should for ourselves and for our families and then put our trust in God, then there is a peace, a deep-down peace, that can sustain us while the world seems to fragment in chaos around us.

One of St Padre Pio's favorite sayings was, "Pray, trust, and don't worry." If, despite everything, we try to raise our hearts and minds to God to offer and surrender ourselves to him without reservation, then this leads on to the total and unconditional trust that opens us as never before to the love Jesus himself received throughout his life on earth. His total trust in the Father to whom he offered and surrendered everything meant that despite all that befell him he was at all times open to his love. Though his mind may have been distracted by serving those who loved him and suffering from those who hated him, his heart was ever open to receive the love that always sustained and never left him. This love was not only received but experienced as it penetrated every part of his human personality.

This is why Jesus is the most secure and mature human being who has ever walked on the face of this earth, and he offers the same security and maturity to those who learn to trust as he did. The sign of this inner security was the profound peace that he experienced

25 - The Feel-Good Factor

deep down within himself despite the storms that raged around him. It was this peace that he promised to his disciples when he met them again after the Resurrection.

The experience of this profound peace is the first tangible sign that the trust that opens a person to the love of God has borne fruit, and will continue to do so, giving ever greater security and maturity. If the price of this trust costs us dearly in terms of human success or material advantage, then it is cheap at that or any other price for that matter. This is the only "feel-good factor" that really matters.

When I lost the job, I had given my life for, had my book turned down half a dozen times and lost more friends than I care to remember, I went into one of the city churches to turn to the only One I could really trust. Kneeling in front of me was my friend the window cleaner. We had both lost our jobs, lost our friends, and lost our status too, but at least we were turning to Some-one who understood us, because he lost all three himself in the end. But he never gave up trusting in the One who raised him up to confound the greed and the power-seeking hypocrisy of the world and confer on those who would do likewise the strength and power to follow him.

26

The one thing necessary

The teacher I admired most was an existentialist who spent his time trying to convert us to his chosen philosophy. Everything he said seemed to make sense but none of the books he recommended did. They were always too difficult for me, even the more popular works. I struggled for weeks trying to understand Kierkegaard's popular masterpiece Purity of Heart. I thought that at least that would be easy enough to understand, but it wasn't. Nevertheless, it wasn't all a waste of time, for its full title, Purity of Heart Is to Will One Thing, has remained with me over the years and helped me to understand things that I may never have understood without it. It has helped me, for instance, to understand what Jesus meant when he said that there is only "one thing necessary."

You see, when you really think about it that is all that really matters, to will one thing before everything else, and for that you need a pure heart, a heart that is not fragmented by a thousand and one desires competing with each other and destroying the peace of mind that we all long for. Whenever I have been in danger of becoming confused by the complexity of the spiritual life, I just remember Kierkegaard and he puts me back on the straight and narrow again. A pure heart is utterly simple because it simply wants one thing. I don't know what that one thing was for Kierkegaard, but for Jesus it is to love God with your whole heart and your

26 - The one thing necessary

whole mind and your whole being. Nothing else matters. If you get this right, then everything else follows as a matter of course. As St. John pointed out, if your love of God is genuine it automatically enables you to love your neighbor, which is the second of the two commandments that sum up all the others. Taken together the two of them constitute what came to be known in the Early Church as the "Great Mandatum of the Lord," possible only to those who had the genuine purity of heart that enabled them to will but one thing in all things.

When Jesus said, "Blessed are the pure of heart for they shall see God," he meant that when you begin to love God above all else you can begin to see him in everything and everyone and encounter him in everything you do and in everyone you meet. In order to do this more perfectly the Desert Fathers used to spend time each morning examining the forthcoming day to see how their single-minded love of God could enable them to trans-form it. They would try to anticipate all that they had to do and the people they would expect to meet, so that throughout that day they could continue to offer themselves to God by the gentle and peaceful way in which they did everything and treated everyone. Success was never gauged by how well they succeeded in doing this but by how well they tried and tried again and again on successive days no matter how often they failed.

St Francis of Assisi used to say that if you can't love your neighbors then at least do not harm them. And let's face it, for most of us that is about the most we can do while we wait on God to give us the grace to do what is quite impossible without it. What the Desert Fathers learned and what St Francis practiced so perfectly was that mere waiting on God is worthless unless that time is filled by doing all we can do to receive the grace to love our neighbor as ourselves. That is why the Desert Fathers spent their time before the day began preparing for it by trying to anticipate all they had to do and everyone they had to meet. Then they asked God's help to enable them to do everything as Jesus himself would have done. They found from experience that this was the best way to extend the purity of heart with which they tried to make their morning offering at the beginning of the day, throughout every moment of that day. This is how they endeavored to observe at all times the "Great Mandatum," what Jesus called the "one thing necessary" without which nothing has any ultimate meaning or purpose.

Thanks to Kierkegaard I was able to see one of the simplest truths of the spiritual life that I may not have seen so clearly without him, and to see too from the practice of the Desert Fathers how that truth can transform each passing day.

27

Who wins a rat-race?

You do not need to be a clairvoyant to predict that the winner of a rat-race is invariably a rat. Alf had won three rat-races in successive years, and this had qualified him to be made 'king rat' with a plum job at headquarters training other would-be rats, otherwise known as super-salesmen. They were so-called because they were superior to the eighty percent of applicants who didn't make the grade, and superior to other salesmen who were en-cumbered with consciences.

Their training had all the hallmarks of a religious cult whose members have to give up everything in order to sell the all-purpose 'Wonder vacuum' with which they will liberate the world from the domestic slavery to which it has been condemned. Every morning the salesmen were taught how to plan each day with a series of 'meditations' that would enable them to set goals or targets for themselves. Then they would solemnly resolve to attain them by the end of that day. If they did not, they were taught to punish themselves with some sort of penance at the end of it, and then confess their failures to their supervisor at the end of the week. Nothing must get in the way of their daily targets, not even the wife. "Ditch the wife" was Alf's favorite aphorism to the "wets" who had whining wives who didn't know what was good for them. He used to delight in explaining to his trainees that they had to sacrifice everything to their calling and for the BMW always awarded to the year's super-rat.

He taught them how to phone potential customers with the words, "I'm just phoning to give you the news that you have been selected to receive the world's most advanced domestic cleaning system absolutely free." I won't tell you how Alf manipulated them into buying what they thought they were getting for free, or you may try to do Alf out of a job and that would not be healthy for either of us.

Jesus was not averse to telling stories like this, not to commend the heroes' morals but their worldly-wise wisdom from which even the children of light could learn. After all you cannot but admire the single-mindedness that enables them to dedicate each day to their cause with such enthusiasm. If only a few of us had the same energy that drives them, we might be able to do for the modern world what the first Christians did for the ancient world. Meanwhile we can learn something from them to our advantage.

What better way to prepare for the day ahead than by setting ourselves goals or targets to attain by the end of it (though I don't particularly like the use of these words that have been soiled by the commercial world and given nuances that I would prefer to avoid). However, once we've offered the day to God and mentally previewed it with the aim of transforming it, it's a good idea to make a few resolutions to do what we are likely to forget or find convenient to forget. It might be just to do hum-drum tasks that we keep putting off, like changing the sheets on the bed, putting air into the car tires, or defrosting the freezer, or something that's more important. There's always that friend or relative who's sick or in need whom we should phone, or write to, or even drop in on for a few minutes. Or perhaps we should make a resolution to apologize to one of the family, a friend or someone at work for the way we behaved the previous day.

27 - Who wins a rat-race?

It is very difficult to stand up for someone who has been abused by authority at work, or elsewhere, or to speak the truth when no one wants to hear it, or to make a stand for what we know is right, but these are some of the more important things that could occupy our minds as part of morning prayer. Then we can ask for the strength to put the resolutions that we know we ought to make into practice. I can't promise you a BMW if you regularly keep your resolutions, but at least I can promise you peace of mind. I can even promise you peace of mind if you fail, as long as you make a genuine attempt to do what is right and sincerely ask God's pardon if you fail.

28

Schola Divini Amoris

I'm afraid I almost gave up prayer for good shortly after I started, because I had so many distractions that I thought it was pointless. When I explained myself to a well-known retreat master, he said he'd been praying seriously for over fifty years and he never come away from prayer without more distractions then he cared to count. Furthermore, he said he never yet met anyone who could pray without any distractions.

He told me that if I could ever say, hand on heart, that I had no distractions at prayer I either have fallen asleep or been lifted up into an ecstasy. In neither case could I say that I had been praying. When you are asleep you are not doing anything and when you are in ecstasy God is doing everything. Prayer is what happens in between the time when you are doing nothing and God is doing everything, and that time is always full of more distractions than we would like.

We all have the strange idea at the back of our minds that when we finally make it in prayer, whatever that may mean, we'll be like the saints who we fondly imagine never had any distractions and were continually lost in profound contemplation and exciting mystical experiences. The difference between us and the saints is not that we have distractions in prayer, and they did not, it is that their distractions were far worse than ours, far stronger than we have ever had. At times they were all but overwhelming. The greater the mystic, the greater the battles that have to be fought in prayer, and the darker the dark nights they have to endure.

Take a look at the prayer of the greatest mystic who has ever walked on the face of this earth. See Jesus at prayer in the desert at the beginning of his public ministry, or in Gethsemane at the end of it, and you'll see him fighting against enormous temptations that would turn him away from the prayer he wanted to make, from the will of the Father he wanted to obey.

Distractions belong to the very essence of prayer. Remember the definition of prayer in the old catechism: "Prayer is the raising of the heart and the mind to God." The very word "raising" implies something that has to be done not once but time and time again. That is why I think that Cardinal Hume put his finger on it when he once said, adding one word to the catechism definition, that "prayer is *trying* to raise the heart and the mind to God," so nobody can be in any doubt, not just that distractions are always there, but that prayer is not really prayer without them. Not only that, but the more there are, and the stronger they are, the more fruitful our prayer can be.

Let us imagine that the next time you go to prayer you have only two distractions. The first lasts for five minutes, as you daydream about the summer holidays you've promised yourself in the Seychelles. The second distraction lasts a full ten minutes, as you try to work out how you'll find the money to get there. Only once or twice at the most in the whole of the fifteen minutes do you say no to the fantasy world you want to enjoy in order to turn to the one you've gone to prayer for in the first place. In fifteen minutes, you manage to perform one or possibly two acts of selflessness. Not even your best friends would give you more than say one or two out of ten for that.

But let's imagine, instead, that you had a hundred and one distractions in fifteen minutes. What would that mean? It would mean that one hundred and one times you had to say no to self and yes to God; a hundred and one times you would have had to act selflessly. Even your worst enemy would have to give you at least seven out of ten for that. That is why the medieval mystic Angela of Foligno said that prayer is the *schola divini amoris,* the school of divine love, the place where you go to learn loving by giving your time and energy to God when you're tempted to give it to yourself time and time again.

If you think about it for a moment or two it makes sense. Not even God can force his love on someone who does not want it, but if you spend all your prayer time trying to turn to him again and again, it's quite obvious what you really do want, and that is when God gives it.

So distractions should not be dismissed as an evil that makes prayer pointless, because they offer us the opportunity of practicing selflessness again and again. In this way they give God the opportunity of giving what he always wants to give to anyone who is open to receive it. What is learned in this school can be put into practice in the wider world to which we all have to return. The love that we have received there can be the salt to give the world savor, the leaven to make it rise.

29

Walking the tightrope

Although I was not particularly pious, I looked forward to the Jesuit retreats that always heralded the first term in the new academic year. I liked the emphasis on human endeavor in the spiritual journey and was so inspired by a particular retreat master that I decided to set about my own sanctification within hours of the retreat ending.

After a month of all-night vigils, sleeping on the floor and hours and hours of prayer, I ended up in the sick bay more than half exhausted. Of course, I'd gone too far. I not only shattered my body but the dreams I had of the sanctity that I thought I could attain for myself by my own efforts. I had fallen into the old heresy of semi-Pelagianism, and fallen out with all my friends, who thought I had become a religious fanatic. They all came back when I became an atheist, resigned from all the sodalities, and settled for socialism instead.

Sometime later when I was struck by an angel of light, or something heavy, I had a sort of conversion experience, but this time I settled for the Dominican approach. It stressed not so much what we can do but rather what God can do if we only allow him to. It seemed to me far more civilized, and far less strenuous for that matter. Instead of resuming all the spiritual high-jinks that I tried before, I decided to give God a chance to do what I tried too hard to do previously. So, I spent most of my prayer time slumped in a pew doing nothing in particular, like a suet pudding waiting to be soaked in syrup. This time I misinterpreted another great spiritual tradition and ended up in Quietism.

I cannot help thinking that the spiritual life's rather like trying to walk on a tightrope, continually falling off at one moment into semi-Pelagianism, at another into Quietism. It is so difficult to get the balance between pride and presumption. When I started studying the great Christian mystics to help me find it, I began to notice how often the words "gentle" or "gently" kept cropping up. It helped me realize not just the arrogance but the violence that dominated my attempts to storm the gates of heaven. I was trying, no doubt about that, but the way I was trying manifested a deep, ingrained pride that guaranteed failure.

It was about this time that I came across this quotation from Simone Weil. "A person is no more than the quality of their endeavour." It was the quality of my endeavour that was all wrong and I saw that I was going nowhere until I got it right. I wrote two words above the start of my five-hundred and fifty-ninth new beginning - "Trying" and "Gently." I didn't want to end up in Quietism again, so the word "Trying" would remind me of the effort I had to put in, while the word "Gently" would help me realize that my endeavour alone would lead me nowhere without God's endeavour.

When I started to pray again in earnest, I had a new definition of prayer to help keep me on the straight and narrow. It was this: "Prayer is the art of gently trying to raise the heart and mind and the whole being to God." Put like that it sounds easy, but having a nice cozy definition of prayer does not guarantee a first-class ticket to the Transforming Union even if it is theologically accurate. It is a help, no doubt about it, but speaking personally I've spent more years of my life than I care to remember falling off that tightrope, first this way and then that. Every time I hear an inspiring sermon, read an uplifting book, or hear of the exploits of the saints I clench my fists, spread my nostrils wide, grind my teeth together and try to summon up all the strength I need to make myself into the new man by my own spiritual muscle power. It always fails and I always find myself back once more flirting with the Quietism that I thought I'd left for good, leaving everything to God and doing nothing for myself.

How does the balance come? It comes gradually through the trial and error of man and the grace and goodness of God. It comes to everyone who has the courage to persevere on that tightrope and the humility to keep getting up to begin again and again, no matter how many times they fall off into pride or into presumption. "When you stop falling you are in heaven, but when you stop getting up you are in hell".

30

The Secret of Success

It's over forty years now since Roger Bannister ran the mile in under four minutes. I was delighted when they showed several reruns of the race on television to mark the occasion. The moment I like best is when he collapses into the arms of his coach, Franz Standfl, seconds after breaking the tape. It's the moment when I can impress my friends by saying, "Look, there's my old coach, Franz Standfl."

I first heard about him in the fifties when I was competing in the national schools' athletics championships at the White City in London. I'm afraid I didn't break any records, in fact I didn't even get a bronze, but I met many boys who did, and they all came from the same school, John Fisher's in Purley. The school carried off more medals than any other and became the overall champions with a massive tally of points. When I asked how they did it they all gave the same answer — "Franz Standfl." He became the school coach only the year before, but in one year he had turned a school with no athletic tradition into the champions of all England. Our school coach was so impressed by what Standfl had been able to achieve in a matter of months that he arranged for our athletics team to spend two weeks at the school to see what he could do for us.

Franz Standfl won the gold medal in the decathlon at the Berlin Olympics in 1936, so it was hardly surprising that he was a master of every athletic event. But what made him so successful was not just his technical know-how, but his knowledge of a method of training that was the secret of his success. Every day, in addition to practising the techniques that he taught, we had to spend several hours weight training in the gym. It was hard and painful, but it made a tremendous difference to our performance. The key to his success was that he could give us the two things necessary for every successful performance. First, he gave us the technical knowledge that we needed, and secondly he gave us the power to transpose that technical knowledge into a winning performance. He explained to us that each time we raised the weights above our heads we were exercising not just the muscles in our arms but the muscles in every part of our body simultaneously.

No one could see as clearly as Franz Standfl that knowledge is not enough without the power to put that knowledge into practice. It was only later, much later, that I came to see and understand that it is exactly the same in the spiritual life. It is not too difficult learning what to do and how to do it, the real problem is finding out how to achieve the power to do it. When I studied the lives of the great spiritual athletes, I saw that they all used the same gymnasium for the training they had in common. They all set aside some time for solitude each day for the prayer in which they raised something far more difficult than heavy weights. They repeatedly raised their hearts and minds to God as they practised the supreme virtue of selfless loving.

When you practise this virtue, you are in fact practising the three most important virtues of all at one and the same time, faith, hope, and charity. When you selflessly try to love the One whom you cannot see or feel or touch, you are exercising the spiritual muscles of your mind that will generate a faith strong enough to move more than mere mountains. And when you try to love that Someone to the exclusion of all else, even though you seem to receive nothing in return, you are exercising the muscles of your heart as never before. Then that heart can learn how to love beyond all human loving, and hope beyond hope until it receives much more than it ever hoped for.

All the other moral virtues, like temperance and fortitude, mentioned in textbooks, are practised repeatedly whenever you attempt this selfless loving. In other words, you are practising fortitude when you must go on giving without apparently receiving anything in return. You are practising temperance too, and that does not come easily to a self-indulgent human being, who would far rather be sitting in front of the television, or drinking in the pub, or dining at the club. These and all the moral virtues are practised automatically as the supreme sacrifice of selflessness is continually offered to God through prayer.

If vices are bad habits, then virtues are good habits that have to be learned and then brought to peak perfection through exercise in the spiritual gymnasium where the heart and mind are raised to God time and time again. That is why prayer is to the ascetic what weightlifting is to the athlete, and that is why the word 'ascetic' is derived from the Greek word for exercise.

Whenever I see Roger Bannister breaking the tape and falling into the arms of Franz Standfl I am reminded of the athlete I never became and of the ascetic I could still become. I know that the muscles of my mind and heart are far too flabby, but I also know that the spiritual gymnasium that I need is always there, always open, inviting me to get back into training, the type of training I need more than any other.

Whenever I find I have strayed over the years, from the prayer I once vowed would always be a part of my daily life, I begin by returning to Fr. Handley's little memory jog 'Pater', and the 'Noster'

30 - The Secret of Success

that I added later. I have always found it very useful because you can carry it around in your head at all times. It can be used before getting up in the morning, or before falling asleep at night, as well as at any convenient moments during the day. However, if this method of prayer is going to deepen as the years go by, it must be harnessed to another form of prayer that has been practiced since the early days of the Church.

This is the prayer that enables a person to pray, not just with Jesus, but in him, and through him, ever more perfectly, as meditation leads on to contemplation. It was this form of prayer that I was first introduced to in the sixth form. Let me explain what I mean if you will allow me to reminisce once more?

31

Blind love

I always used to look forward to Friday mornings during the school holidays. Mrs Allsop would come at nine o'clock on the dot to help my Mother 'do' the house. If my brothers were at home too, we would all linger in anticipation on the upstairs landing, waiting for Mrs Allsop's familiar catchphrase that would send us into hysterics. The merest mention of an upset or the most minor disaster was enough to start her off: "In't it awful, Mrs. Torkington — Oooh, in't it awful?"

It wasn't just the sameness or the predictability of her response, or even the remarkable cadences of her "Ooohs", that got us going, but her priceless accent that literally had us rolling in fits of laughter. It was half-Mancunian and half-Parisian, the reason being that Mrs Allsop was married to a teacher who taught French at a local grammar school.

They had been pen pals, trying to improve their knowledge of the other's language. To begin with they hardly wrote to each other more than once a month, then it was once a week, then it was almost every day. The more they came to know each other the more they came to love each other, and their decision to marry was made before they actually met. Time proved it was the right decision. It was not a unique case. I have come across many other examples since, in real life as well as in literature.

You do not have to see someone to get to know them well enough to fall in love with them, though of course it is far easier if you can meet them face to face. That is why Jesus said, "Blessed are they who have not seen and yet have learned to believe." This was not just a rebuke to Thomas and the other disciples whose faith had recently proved a little wobbly at the knees, but a genuine tribute to the followers, including us, who would have to learn how to know him and love him without seeing him.

The story of how the Allsops came to know and love each other not only moved me, but it also made me believe that it was possible to know and love somebody without seeing them. At the time I was deeply moved to read how the Desert Fathers had learned to love the Christ whom they had never seen by slowly reading and meditating on every word that he said and every action that he performed, as well as what others had said about him.

Four words have been traditionally used to describe the pattern of Christian prayer that first flourished in the desert before it extended its influence to the rest of Christendom. The words are *Lectio, Meditatio, Oratio* and *Contemplatio*. The Desert Fathers' search for Christ would begin with the slow, reverent reading of the divinely inspired texts (*lectio*), often preceded by a prayer to the Holy Spirit to allow them to be uplifted by the same Spirit who inspired the sacred texts in the first place. Then they would mull over in their minds what they had read (*meditatio*), until they were moved to respond in their own words to the One who spoke to them through the Scriptures (*oratio*). Gradually a profound spiritual dialogue would take place under the influence of the Holy Spirit, that led to a deep inner silence.

Like the natural mystic who experiences God's presence through his 'words written' in the beauty of creation, the Christian mystics who experience God's 'words written' in the beauty of his Master Creation are led into a deep interior stillness in which they just want to rest, replete with what they have received. Now, when everything has been said that needs to be said, they just want to gaze with an awe-ful loving attention upon the One whose words they have received (*contemplatio*).

This pattern of prayer that first developed with the monks in the desert was followed by other Christians and became the norm for all who wanted to seek and find what the monks had found in their desert solitude. As time passed, some would write down their own personal meditations, as St Augustine did in his Confessions. Other 'confessions' or personal meditations followed. Then others would write down the prayers that were the fruit of their meditations. The anthologies of the meditations and prayers of the spiritual masters that resulted were used by the faithful, together with the Scriptures, to lead them to the prayer that flowers in contemplation, where the Unseen is 'seen' with the eye of faith, and in profound spiritual experiences. These experiences were described and explained by the great mystical writers in subsequent centuries.

I have Mrs. Allsop to thank for teaching me how the Unseen can be 'seen' and embraced through words laden with love. I have her to thank too for teaching me a little humility the day she handed in her notice. "Nothing personal," she said to my mother. "I've given in my notice to all my employers. I think I have enough material now." "Material for what?" asked my mother. "For my doctoral thesis," she replied, "on the manners and mores of the English middle classes!"

32

Love in Lourdes

I was smitten by my first romantic infatuation on the school pilgrimage to Lourdes. Her name was Maria. She was one of about twenty Italian girls staying in the same hotel as us. She was stunning. She had the most beautiful olive skin you could imagine, long dark hair and big brown eyes. I was only fourteen; she must have been at least a year older than me. I can't remember much about that pilgrimage. I can only remember Maria. I can only remember following her down to the grotto, in and out of the basilica, to the Blessed Sacrament chapel and back to the hotel again, several times over!

I never said a word to her. We did not even exchange glances. She would not have been interested in a pimply beanpole like me anyway. But I did dream about her once, and I daydreamed about her all the time. I dreamt about her loving me as I loved her. I might not have got much spiritual benefit from that pilgrimage, but my amorous experience did help me to understand the bishop's sermon at the farewell Mass.

He said that God loves us more than we will ever know and pursues us like a "hound of heaven" and will continue to pursue us until we love him in return with our whole hearts and minds and with our whole beings. Although I thought it a bit odd calling God a "hound of heaven," it reminded me of the way I had been following Maria along the highways and byways of Lourdes and it helped me to understand a little better how God must feel, loving me without receiving any love in return. But after what I felt for Maria, I could not imagine I would ever be able to love God as I loved her, with my whole heart, my whole mind and with my whole being. God seemed so distant, so far away, so abstract to love, as I had come to understand the word.

After three more 'love affairs' in as many years, I tried to explain how I felt to a priest who seemed very understanding. He said, "That is precisely why God became man so that we could love him in Jesus." I didn't have the courage to tell him that I did not quite like the idea of loving another man, even if he was the Son of God. It may do for girls, but it would not do for me. So, I left him as mystified as when I went to see him. Loving God was far too difficult for me, so I decided to stick to girls instead.

Then I came across an article on spirituality in a copy of a magazine called *The Way*. It seemed to resolve all the difficulties. It said that in the Old Testament God was sometimes called a Mother as well as a Father and endowed with feminine as well as masculine characteristics. It explained how some of the Fathers of the Church spoke of what they called the anima and the animus in God. In other words, God is neither male nor female, but the qualities of maleness and femaleness can be found perfectly balanced in him. They are not only balanced in him but brought to perfection in the ultimate quality of love that St. Paul said surpasses our understanding.

If this love is to be found to perfection in the perfect man Jesus Christ, then the transcendental and supra-sexual quality of his love is belied by his obvious maleness. The animus and the anima that are found to perfection in God can also be found to perfection in him and in the quality of his loving. That is why in responding to his loving, men and women can respond equally, if differently, and both ultimately find their completion in him and in each other. Here alone will they find a total sexual equality where there is "no more marrying or giving in marriage," because the love that is symbolized in the sacrament is brought to perfection in the love of God that is beyond our understanding, but not beyond our desiring. It can be glimpsed, albeit briefly, in this life through the love of the "Perfect Man" and through the love of any man and woman for each other when their love is pure and selfless.

That article in *The Way* resolved for me what had been unresolved before and opened not one but two possible directions for me to take on my journey to the fulness of love that I desired more than anything else. At last, I could see that the love of God was now open to me because it could be found fully embodied in Jesus Christ. The ambiguity about loving him that held me back before no longer restrained me.

Perhaps that pilgrimage to Lourdes was not a waste of time after all. I did not see any cures taking place. I did not witness any miracles, but I did glimpse in a very distant and obscure way the greatest miracle of all!

33

Thanks to my lucky stars

I was having a totally normal conversation with a complete stranger at a Christmas party until he asked me what I did for a living. When I told him he suddenly changed, started squirming and smiling in a most odd way and said, "Have you been saved, brother?"

Without a moment's hesitation I said, "Yes."

"And when did it happen?" he asked.

"In 1956," I said, "thanks to Bill Haley and the Comet."

I was not trying to be funny, or to put him down. The words just came out of my mouth without my thinking about it. But it was true. I had been saved by Bill Haley and the Comets, saved from the social isolation that I thought was threatening to turn me into a permanent bachelor. You see, I simply could not master ballroom dancing, apart from the waltz, and I could only do that in straight lines, so I did not bother to do anything at all. It was embarrassing enough to have to say to a beautiful young woman, "May I have the pleasure of this dance?" knowing full well it would be no pleasure at all for her, so I just sat the evening out, hoping they would play the 'Gay Gordons'.

Bill Haley and the rock revolution that followed in his wake changed all that. Now I could stand up with anyone and make a ridiculous exhibition of myself, throwing my body all over the place, and end up applauded as the best dancer in the room. If it was not for rock'n'roll I would never have met Petrina, never have fallen head over heels in love with her, never have known what heaven on earth really felt like.

In those days heaven on earth cost little by today's standards. It did not even cost me the bus fare to take her home. We walked there hand in hand, one hour and twenty minutes of unalloyed bliss, and I did not even have a kiss at the end of it.

I hated going back to boarding school with only letters to fan the flames. It took me several weeks before I could drag myself back to the Monday meditation group and even then, my mind was elsewhere. But when Father Handley said that God is love and all human love is nothing compared with the divine, I sat up and began to take notice. If I could not have the human until the summer holidays, I decided to seek the divine and try to find out whether what he said was true or not. I remember coming across a quotation from William of St. Thierry that said, "You cannot love someone unless you know them, but you'll never know them unless you love them." My brief 'love affair' with Petrina enabled me to see the truth of what he said, and so I began to try out a method of prayer that promised to lead me through knowledge to the fulness of love that filled Jesus Christ.

It was a modern presentation of the method of prayer used by the Desert Fathers, called the "Four R's." First you had to READ the sacred texts and then reread them slowly and prayerfully. Then you had to REFLECT on what you had read, ruminate, as St. Augustine would say, on the inner meaning of every word, to let those words seep deep down into the very marrow of your being. Then you had to REACT in your own way, in your own words. Real prayer began as you started to raise your heart and mind to God. When everything had been said that needed to be said, then the whole being would enter a state of deep REPOSE. This was no longer a time for reading or reflecting, or even for responding to what had been read, but for being still, for being at rest.

It took me a long time to get going, but the love I had already experienced made me hunger for more and more of the same, and so I was spurred on to give as much time as I could each day to the practice of the "Four R's." Gradually I was touched and moved to react in the language of love to what I had read. Sure enough, when all had been said that I wanted to say, it became easy and pleasant to pause and gaze with the eyes of faith at the One whose presence I felt I experienced enveloping my whole being.

If pressed, I would have to admit it was only second best to holding hands with Petrina, but it was much more than I had ever imagined possible. I have no doubt that I would have believed I had been "saved" if I'd been brought up in another tradition. As it was, I merely believed I had arrived at the heights of mystic union. I thought I had reached the top of Mount Tabor, when in fact I'd hardly penetrated the foothills. I had a long, long way to go and, truth to tell, I still have.

If I am finally saved, though I won't know 'till I get there, I'm going to seek out Bill Haley and his Comets and say, "thank you." If it wasn't for them, I may well have spent my whole life skulking around in those dreaded ballrooms, waiting for the 'Gay Gordons'. I may never have known what heaven on earth was really like and may never have desired the real thing.

34

When sparks first flicker into flame

The first six weeks of that summer holiday were heaven on earth. I was either with Petrina, dreaming of her or talking about her. The last two weeks were hell on earth. She waited until the last minute to tell me that she was leaving school earlier than had been anticipated to follow her father into the forces to become an army nurse.

On my return to school, I abandoned the meditation that had kept me going the previous term, to beg God, or anyone else up there to keep her heart burning, as my heart burned for her, and to keep her letters flowing, as mine flowed to her. But they became little more than a trickle as autumn turned to winter when they froze up completely, and so did my heart. Someone in the place where marriages are made had evidently decided that the one, I had in mind would not be made there. I longed to do something dramatic, like enter a monastery, join the foreign legion, or make some other futile gesture, but I knew it would only be a waste of time, and she would probably never know about it anyway.

Almost a year after I thought I had reached the mystic heights I decided to re-scale them and try to find there at least some sparks of the love I would by choice have chosen to find elsewhere. This time I turned to meditation manuals for my inspiration. They had grown in popularity when fewer and fewer people were able to understand the Latin into which the Scriptures had been translated, and when translations by reformers tended to favour interpretations that were frowned on by the 'established Church.' But I soon found that even the most modern were either too dry and rational or too pious and sentimental for my palate, and so I returned to the Scriptures as before. I would have chosen to follow the exercises of St. Ignatius which have been one of the most successful means of systematic meditation since the Reformation, but they needed a spiritual director and thirty days in which to follow them. So, I had to make do with some suggestions adapted from them by Fr. Bassett SJ who directed the school retreat that year.

The idea was to set the scene in your imagination before beginning your meditation, to picture in detail the surroundings in which the events that you were about to consider were going to take place. If it was the Last Supper, you had to paint the scene in your mind, see the disciples preparing the room, setting the table, laying the food out for Jesus and the rest of his disciples. Then you had to look at their faces as they came in the door, gaze upon the countenance of Jesus as he took his place at table and see the expression on his face. Then, beginning to read his words from the sacred texts, you would pore over every nuance as the most profound dialogue that has ever taken place begins to unfold.

Some did not find this sort of approach particularly helpful; others with more imaginative minds did. I did, at least for a time. It helped create the sort of inner environment that made meditation easier and more enjoyable and led me back to prayer more quickly than I thought possible, as I began to respond in my own words to the words of Jesus. I was taught to take his words as addressed not just to the disciples but to me personally, so that they could do for me what they did for his followers.

The school spiritual director insisted that methods of meditation are

34 - When sparks first flicker into flame

no more than the means to lead a person to gaze upon love made flesh, not just to be inspired by what is seen, but to experience what is seen reaching out to touch them. When onlookers experience the touch of love, they are onlookers no longer but become participators in a process of giving and receiving that gradually transforms the receiver into the giver. This is a gradual transformation that takes place not in weeks, or even months but in years of painful purifications.

But to begin with, when the first sparks begin to flicker into a flame, they ignite into what is predominantly an emotional experience that is called 'first fervour'. Like so many others who are first enveloped by this honeymoon stage of prayer, I thought I had reached the heights and would therefore be able to lead and guide others to the spiritual peaks that I thought I had attained. I had no idea at the time of the incredible arrogance and pride that fermented deep down within me. It was hidden from view beneath a thin coat of spiritual fervor that made me burn with a religious enthusiasm that deceived all but the wise and the cynical.

No wonder my prayers had not been answered. The place where marriages are made obviously intended to save the person, I thought I loved from a fate far worse than becoming an army nurse'.

35

The fallen idol

It was extremely difficult for a dyslexic like me to choose a career in those days, especially as I had a congenital aversion to all forms of manual work. All the professions that required examinations and all the jobs that demanded physical labor had to be ruled out as a matter of course, so I had been seriously considering the stage, when a career as a spiritual guru presented itself to me quite out of the blue.

I would not in the normal way of things have thought of searching for God's love through prayer, if I was able to find it through the love of the girl who left me to become an army nurse. But I found myself bereft and loveless in a boarding school, where you were more likely to meet a Martian than a member of the opposite sex. I therefore transferred all the pent-up energy that I had been reserving for the girl who had chosen to leave me, to the God who promised to be with me always.

I dedicated my spare time to meditation, and this gradually became easier as the sparks of love for the person I began to discover in the Scriptures soon flickered into a flame that burned more brightly the more I persevered. My meditation received a shot in the arm from my reading of Archbishop Goodier's Life of Christ, as well as a small meditation manual he wrote that I found more helpful than any other I came across. The meditations consisted of a few words, a phrase, or a brief sentence or two taken from the Scriptures and these fanned the sparks into a flame that soon began to burn throughout the whole period of prayer.

Suddenly, what had at first been difficult and arduous became easy and enjoyable. I could honestly say, "Lord it is good for me to be here," and I wanted to stay there permanently, as the disciples had wanted to stay with Jesus on Mount Tabor. I gathered from my spiritual reading that I had arrived at what is called Contemplation, when words no longer have the importance or meaning that they had before because you just want to gaze in loving attention upon the One who had formerly seemed so distant, so far away.

There were similarities with the mystical experiences I had before, when I was spellbound by the beauty of the natural world around me, but now different features became apparent. What were rare and brief experiences before now became almost literally the order of the day each time I went to prayer. The One whom I had experienced as 'out there' not only seemed close by but seemed to enter into my inmost being to possess me from the inside.

The natural mystical experiences that had first made me 'wonder' seemed to draw me together as one and made me yearn for the 'beyond' in what I saw or heard around me. It seemed to be a supra-emotional experience that predominantly engaged my mind. The new contemplative gaze that drew me together grew out of systematic meditations on the 'beyond' made present in the Masterwork of God's creation, Jesus Christ. As the 'beyond' was now clothed in his human flesh and blood, it drew out a human response that touched the feelings and emotions that had not been touched in the natural mystical experiences that first moved me. Now it was not only my mind, but my emotions too that were drawn together as one and directed to the 'One' who emerged from the margins to become the centre of my life.

The still, silent, contemplative gaze was similar to what it was before, but now it could be attained and sustained by human emotions and feelings. Whereas the natural mystical experience always tended to generate humility in the experience of the ultimately unattainable, this new contemplative experience tended to generate pride because the unattainable seemed attainable by human endeavour. This is why later mystical writers called the high point of first fervour, "Acquired Contemplation," to allay unwarranted pride and the mistaken assumption that true "Mystical Contemplation," which they may or may not receive later, is anything other than a pure gift of God.

Nevertheless, in the fullness of his adolescent ignorance, yours truly arrogantly believed he had reached the heights of the spiritual life and set about looking for disciples to gather around him to whom he could impart the higher wisdom he thought he had most recently attained. His theatrical pretensions came to his aid as he was able to simulate saintly traits and characteristics to leave his disciples in no doubt that he was who he pretended to be. Had an unbeliever from the fifth form not call him a, "bloody hypocrite" in front of his disciples, and received a bloody nose for his pains, who knows, Holy Mother Church might well have welcomed a new religious order into her ranks.

36

Into the dark night

When a violent display of bad temper finally convinced my would-be disciples that I was not the guru for them, I turned to the school spiritual director in the hope that he, at least, would be able to see the genuine sanctity beneath my 'justified anger'. Of course, he must have been impressed by the speed of my spiritual ascent, but he didn't show it. He merely insisted that I should continue as before to give time each day to the fervent 'contemplative prayer' that had become my daily joy.

As the spiritual immaturity of my fellow students had prevented me from founding the religious order I had intended, I was forced to join someone else's at the end of the school year. The novitiate could have been far more fruitful for all concerned if it had only been organized by me instead of the priest whom I considered spiritually quite out of his depths. Prudence dictated that I should ignore him and choose instead to submit myself in all humility to my own spiritual direction, with the help of some of the spiritual masters whose books could be found in the novitiate library. I was deeply moved by one book in particular. It was by the Cistercian, Eugene Boylan and called *This Tremendous Lover*. It spurred me on to give more and more time to the prayer that was always filled with sweetness and light.

Then suddenly something happened quite out of the blue. It was as if someone had turned out the lights and left me in the dark. Prayer was no longer sweet, but dry and arid. All the fervour that had fired me before fired me no more. I was in a black, black hole, and try as I might I could not get out of it.

I thought it was just a temporary blackout and that sweetness and light would resume in a day or too, but it did not. Things finally got so bad that I had to swallow my pride and seek help from the novice master whom I had dismissed as no more than a novice himself. He explained how what had happened to me had also happened to him, as it does to everyone when first fervor fizzles out. I was naturally outraged. I was not in my first fervour, nor was I like everyone else. I was a mystic who had reached the heights. I did not go back to him or anyone else for that matter. It was quite evident that that novitiate had nothing to offer me. If I wanted to get anywhere on the spiritual journey, I'd have to get there by myself.

As the months passed without the return of my first fervour, I began wondering what it was all about and what I was doing, giving myself to a God who now seemed to care for me no more than the girl who had walked out on me. I still wanted him, I still yearned for him, but I began to think I would soon get over him, as I got over her.

But I did not. The sort of yearning for God, that I briefly experienced after those natural mystical experiences that had touched me in the past, returned to haunt me permanently. God, it seemed, had left me, but not without leaving me with a deep desire that made me moon around like a young man in love with love, who does not know where to find it. I felt drawn to prayer and returned regularly to where I had so much joy before, but there was no more joy to be found now. Instead, I experienced a thousand and one distractions that cut and thrust at my mind from the inside and made me feel

36 - Into the dark night

I was wasting my time waiting on the God who obviously became fed up waiting on me. The wonderful meditations that had moved me before no longer did so, nor did the Scriptures, nor did the poems or the prayers that moved me in the past. When I arrived at the student house, I tried all the priests I found approachable. They all seemed to understand what had happened to me, but not what was happening, nor what would or should happen in the future.

Then, after months of flicking through spiritual tomes in the library, I came across a book that made sense of everything, well, almost everything. It was called simply *Prayer* by B C Butler, Abbot of Downside. In the appendix entitled 'Mystical Prayer' it explained exactly what had happened to me. It explained why meditation had left me, why my prayer had left me too, and why even God seemed to have left me. But, as it's an ill wind that blows no good, it promised that my pride would gradually leave me, if I had the courage to journey on through the darkness and into "Mystical Contemplation."

Though what he meant by that I had no idea. Not "Mystical Contemplation," you understand. I knew all about that. But what did he mean by pride? What pride? Whose pride? Surely not mine. He may have known a lot about prayer, but he evidently didn't know much about me — that's for sure?

37

The Cloud of Understanding

I must have been an insufferable bore to live with when I was going through my spiritual adolescence, misinterpreting first fervor for the mystic heights. I interpreted the spiritual feelings that I generated to mean that I had been especially chosen by God to lead and guide others. My pathetic presumption made me believe that I was inspired by the 'Spirit of God' instead of the spirit of pride and prejudice that still ruled me as before, beneath all the froth.

I hate to think how I would have continued to delude myself and others if my first fervour had not come to a sudden end, leaving me alone and bereft in a spiritual desert far from the oasis that I thought was destined to be my permanent dwelling place. If a good library had not given me access to the great spiritual masters during my time in the desert, I would surely have given up prayer permanently, like so many others who do not receive the help and support they need. This is the most critical point in spiritual development when an adolescent is called upon to grow up and become an adult. In the days before the Vatican Council a person like me had to pass through their spiritual adolescence in the privacy and seclusion of a personal prayer life. After the Council many passed through it in the company of others, who were on the same spiritual journey, thanks to the charismatic movement.

37 - The Cloud of Understanding

The movement was not new. It first manifested itself in the Early Church when, not surprisingly, whole communities were passing through their first fervor simultaneously, manifesting some of the same, or similar, psychosomatic features that have been shown in subsequent centuries, as Monsignor Ronald Knox has described in his epic work, *Enthusiasm*. Few, if any other movements for renewal have been able to reach out to everyone in quite the same way as charismatic renewal which, with good and mature leadership, can be a powerful force for good. However, as it is a movement for beginners, it is only to be expected that its participants will fall a prey to illusions of spiritual grandeur that always affect those passing through their first fervour. I for one had more than my fair share of them.

These illusions can be compounded when the effect of group emotion results in psychosomatic phenomena that are all too easily given unwarranted theological interpretations, where psychological interpretations would be more appropriate. But if the emotions that are generated in first fervour should not be misinterpreted, neither must they be misunderstood, for they play a vital part in spiritual growth in the Christian tradition. They help support, sustain, and direct the desire for the love of God that finds its most perfect human embodiment in Jesus Christ. The longer the emotions can support and sustain spiritual adolescents, helping them to remain fixed and focused on what is desired more than anything else, then the sooner that desire can be drawn beyond those human emotions into a profound union with the Spirit of God, which resides most perfectly in the Spirit of Christ. When this happens, adolescence ends abruptly, as it did for me, and there can be no going back to the fervour that sustained them before. They either go forward through obscure mystical contemplation into spiritual maturity, or, like the vast majority, pack up regular personal prayer altogether because they do not understand what has happened to them and they cannot find anyone who does.

The only way forward then is to give the same time to prayer that they gave previously, though they get nothing but darkness from what gave them so much light before. Now at least their very presence will demonstrate more clearly than ever before that they are there for God alone, not for what they receive from him, for they seem to receive nothing but a desire that is regularly thwarted, and an inner emotional turmoil that they cannot control.

Methods of prayer that were used before will no longer be of any help. New methods that lead on and into contemplative prayer must now be used to control the turmoil within, while helping the heart's deepest desire to remain fixed "in naked intent" on the God who seems so far away. No one will travel far through this obscure contemplation without help. I found help in the library; in a book I had never heard of until then. If it was not for *The Cloud of Unknowing*, I would never have understood what was happening to me, and how I should journey on in the obscure contemplation that had all but turned me off prayer for good?

38

The prayer of incompetence

I was nineteen when I arrived at the novitiate. Matthew was only fourteen and a half. It was hardly an environment that encouraged human growth, so poor Matthew's psychological development came to a sudden halt. Though the regime at the house of studies was far more liberal, it assumed rather than encouraged the human growth that poor Matthew so badly needed. He was almost thirty by the time he found himself in the sort of environment in which human growth could begin again where it had been arrested fifteen years before.

He was a student, interestingly enough, studying psychology at Southampton University when it happened. Suddenly he began to go through the adolescence that he never experienced as a teenager. He knew exactly what was happening to him and wasn't at all perturbed when people laughed at the clothes he wore, the ridiculous beard he grew, the old banger he drove, and the scrapes he got himself into with students ten years his junior. His emotional development was years behind the intellectual development that enabled him to see clearly that the one had to catch up with the other before he could attain the sort of human maturity that had been denied him in the past. When that happened, he was able to begin his life again, making new decisions about his future that could not have been made before. The last I heard of him was that he was happily married with several children, lecturing at a university somewhere in Scandinavia.

The psychological principle exemplified in this story is generally accepted. If a person has not passed through their adolescence at the appropriate time, they must pass through it at some later time if they would journey on into a fuller maturity. This important stage in human development cannot be bypassed. If a person fails to pass through it, then they will remain a permanent adolescent or pre-adolescent. The same principle holds good for spiritual growth. Spiritual adolescence may often be triggered by some sort of conversion experience and can take place at any age, and for people in every walk of life. Charismatic renewal is a good example of this. There you will find the young, the middle-aged and the old, lay people, religious and priests, all supporting each other as they pass through their spiritual adolescence on their journey towards a deeper spiritual maturity.

Naturally spiritual adolescents do not like being told they are only beginners. I once gave a fellow student a bloody nose for suggesting I was one and dismissed anyone who dared to suggest that my first fervour was anything other than the direct action of the same Spirit who inspired the Man whom I'd committed myself to follow. Thank God I had a wise spiritual director, who never attempted to disillusion me. He just patiently led me on to the place where Someone would do what my pride prevented him from doing. He knew that if he could only keep me faithful to the daily prayer of sweetness and light for long enough, then the powerful emotions that moved me would eventually act like a springboard, enabling my deepest desire to reach out to the pure otherworldly love that was quite beyond them.

Some mystical writers use the word 'ligature' to describe the way in which a person's deepest desire becomes first fixed and then fas-

38 - The prayer of incompetence

tened to the God who can now be reached only through a strange, obscure contemplation in which the emotions have no part. This experience of 'ligature' is at first identical to the natural mystical experience, though it eventually becomes far more regular and reliable and reaches remarkable degrees of intensity.

Now a new type of prayer must be learned that I will describe in more detail later. It is sometimes called 'the prayer of naked intent' or the 'prayer of faith', or 'the prayer of incompetence', as Cardinal Hume described it in his book *Searching for God*. In this prayer the pride of beginners is gradually done to death as they have to learn just how incompetent they are in the way of obscure contemplation which is now the only way forward. A person becomes competent enough to guide and lead others in the spiritual life only after persevering for years in the 'prayer of incompetence', where humility is gradually learned and a totally new experience of God's presence unfolds, that they would never have dreamt possible before.

When I failed to find another spiritual director to replace the man who taught me so much at school, I turned once more to the library and discovered the writings of Dom John Chapman. His letters were a source of great help and encouragement to me, as they have been to many others over the years who, like me, could not find it elsewhere.

39

The enemy within

I don't remember street parties at the end of the war. We certainly didn't have one, but we had the biggest bonfire I'd ever seen, and we had jelly and blancmange, treacle toffee and toffee apples, too. It was fabulous, and so was the war. I was sorry when it was over. I loved sitting glued to the wireless, listening to the reports of the Allied advances and of one victory after another. I was only a very small boy at the time, but the war had a deep and lasting effect on me quite other than the one it should have had. Most boys like fighting anyway, but none more than me. All my heroes were great generals, such as Alexander the Great, my favorite. The greatest nations were the best fighters, like the Ancient Greeks and, most of all, the Spartans.

Even my favourite birds were birds of prey and the best of them all was the peregrine falcon, faster than any other and able to kill other birds twice its size. That's why I loved the weasel too. I was told it was the fiercest animal in the world for its size, and it could kill animals three times its own size with a death grip which could not be broken. It would just hang on and on until it won. That impressed me so much that I made its method my own and won fight after fight with other boys by holding them in headlocks that I would never release until I was victorious. I cannot count the number of fights I fought before my conversion in the sixth form. Fr Bassett said that the real fight has to be fought within. If we could only defeat the enemy within then there'd be peace not only in us but in the whole of the world. He told us that the only weapon with which this victory could be won was the 'sword of the spirit' and that could be wielded only in prayer. This made me turn to prayer with far greater enthusiasm than ever before. If the only fight that really mattered for me and for the world was the fight within, and prayer was the only way to victory, then I'd hang on in prayer come what may, like the weasel, until I was victorious.

I needed that determination to begin with when I had no idea what prayer was all about. It gave me the will to find out, and the will to persevere, come what may. I did not need much determination when things began to go well, and first fervour swept me off my feet. It raised my deepest desires from the grubby things that had once occupied them on to a higher plane, where they just wanted to be occupied by God and God alone. I was ready to undergo whatever hardship was asked of me, whatever sacrifice had to be made, and fight even unto death for what I knew mattered more than anything else. So, I was a little disappointed by how easy prayer became and how easily the victory I thought I'd won had come to me.

I didn't know then what lay ahead. If I had known, I think I would have quit when I thought I was winning. I would not have had to face the real battles that had to be fought when every comfort was taken away from me, and I had to fight on against overwhelming odds, in a darkness I'd never known before. If it was not for the memory of happier days and the promise I made to hang on till the death like the weasel, I would surely have given up. When the emotions of first fervour had rocketed my deepest desires far beyond themselves, and then into what seemed like a dark cloud of unknowing, I needed all the determination of the weasel to stay on course. Then I discovered what the 'prayer of faith' was when I had nothing but faith and faith alone to support the desire for

God, where so many wonderful spiritual feelings and emotions had supported me before.

I think I could have borne the darkness if it had not been for the fight, I'd always been spoiling for over the years; a fight that now had to be fought against all the powers of evil that rose up from within to taunt me, in the spiritual desert where I now found myself. A new form of prayer had to be learned before the weasel lost his grip, and I found it in the nick of time, or rather it was found for me. It was the 'Prayer of the Heart' used by the Desert Fathers who had been where I now found myself many years before.

My attitude to war and violence has changed over the years, but I still have a soft spot for the weasel. If it had not taught me the lesson of a lifetime, I may never have learned it elsewhere.

40

The prayer of the heart

My brother was overjoyed when the Abbot of Mount St. Bernard accepted his request to join the community as a Cistercian monk. However, the Abbot insisted that he should finish his studies at the Sorbonne before he entered the novitiate. If my brother had prayed hard before, now he prayed twice as hard, and haunted the abbey whenever he had a few days to spare.

Prayer seemed to transform him into a new person, full of fervour and enthusiasm. He'd found heaven on earth and thought it would last forever. Eight months later he found that nothing on earth lasts forever, not even heaven. He came home for Christmas, down in the dumps, and nothing anyone could say or do could cheer him up. As soon as Christmas was over, he was off to Mount St. Bernard's to see the novice master, who had been acting as his spiritual director since his acceptance.

Once again, he was a changed man when he returned, not full of fervour this time but full of enthusiasm to return to the prayer he'd been neglecting since what was once full of fire had suddenly turned to ashes. The novice master explained that what happens to all monks who take their calling seriously had happened to him, even before he'd entered the monastery, as it also happens to many other lay people without them understanding what has happened.

He told him that his deep-seated desire for God that had previously been sustained and strengthened by his feelings and emotions had reached out beyond them, drawn by the love that surpasses all understanding. Now he would have to learn a new form of prayer that would enable him to journey onwards by faith alone through dark and obscure contemplation into the 'Light."

He explained that the heart's desire for God, that is nourished in prayer, is like a spaceship. In order to get the craft moving towards its destination, canisters of fuel have to be fitted to act as boosters, to raise it off the ground through the atmosphere and beyond the world where gravity had made it earthbound. Once this has happened the canisters of fuel not only may but must be jettisoned, or they would impede its progress towards its destination. The closer the spaceship comes to that destination the more it comes under the magnetic pull of the planet that draws it faster and faster towards itself.

In prayer, it is the feelings of first fervour that act like boosters to raise the person's deepest desire up and beyond the emotions towards the God who is a Spirit and who must be worshipped 'in Spirit and in Truth'. His love gradually becomes like an ever more powerful magnetic force that draws the heart relentlessly onward. When the feelings and emotions that moved it before no longer move it they have to be abandoned, along with all the forms of prayer that depended upon them in the past.

The novice master told him that although the Desert Fathers knew nothing about spaceships, they knew a lot about the new form of prayer that had to be taught to the young monks when they passed through and beyond the fervour that drew them into the desert in the first place. It was called "The Prayer of the Heart." To those of us who have been brought up in the West, the heart symbolizes the seat of the feelings and emotions, but for the Desert Fathers steeped in the Scriptures, the heart is the center of the whole person.

"The Prayer of the Heart," then, is the prayer that tries to gather together the restless heart that the young monks experience at the beginning of the mystic way, and to direct it to the One who is already drawing them gently towards himself. This prayer will not only help them at the beginning of the mystic way, but it will support and sustain them throughout it, and will take different forms as the journey unfolds. As meditation is no longer possible, and as concentration is difficult to maintain at the best of times, "The Prayer of the Heart" usually consists of no more than a word, a phrase or, at the most, a short sentence. My brother was given "The Jesus Prayer" to recite, one of the best-known forms of The Prayer of the Heart, that had its origin in the wisdom of the Desert Fathers.

I remember very clearly the enthusiasm with which he taught it to me. "Jesus, Son of God, have mercy on me a sinner." It had to be repeated slowly and prayerfully over and over again. Its purpose was to keep the heart's desire fixed and focused on God, whilst helping to still the restlessness within. I did not find it of any help at the time. I was too busy enjoying the fruits of first fervor; my time had not yet come. But when it did, and I had failed to find any prayer to help me in my restlessness, I suddenly remembered my brother and the novice master who helped him. Once again, I returned to the library to seek the help I needed from the wisdom of the Desert Fathers, who had helped my brother in his hour of need.

41

Philokalia

One of the first books I came across in my search for the wisdom of the desert was a work entitled *Writings from the Philokalia*. It particularly caught my attention because of its subtitle, "On Prayer of the Heart." That is exactly what I wanted to know more about, in the hope that it would help support me in the dry spiritual desert in which I found myself. The Greek word "Philokalia" means "love of what is beautiful or good," and this book is an anthology of Orthodox spirituality going back to the Desert Fathers. It was compiled towards the end of the eighteenth century by St Macarius of Corinth and edited by St Nicodemus of the Holy Mountain.

In the Orthodox tradition spirituality is known as hesychasm, a word derived from the Greek and meaning 'stillness or tranquillity'. A hesychast may be a lay person, a hermit or a religious, who chooses to enter into a deep interior stillness in a monastery, in a hermitage, or in their own home, where they can practise "The Prayer of the Heart."

The Prayer of the Heart is a prayer of the whole person, the united person who prays, in the words of St. John Climacus, "with the whole heart, that is with the whole body and soul and spirit." It involves what is called "pure prayer" that is free of images and concepts so important in the Western tradition for all forms of prayer that depend on the use of the emotions and discursive reasoning. It goes without saying that The Prayer of the Heart or pure prayer is ideal for the person who has passed through and beyond first fervour or spiritual adolescence and is at the outset of the Mystic Way, when all forms of prayer involving the feelings and the emotions are of no help, and indeed are even a hindrance if one tries to return to them.

The best-known expression of The Prayer of the Heart is "The Jesus Prayer," as it was first called by St. John Climacus who wrote about it in his spiritual masterpiece, The Ladder of Divine Ascent. He lived the life of a hermit for forty years before becoming the Abbot of the famous monastery on Mount Sinai, so he knew exactly what he was talking about when it came to prayer. He did not, however, lay down a precise formula for The Jesus Prayer, and it has had different variations in the East, though we in the West have come to know it as "Jesus, Son of God, have mercy on me a sinner."

All variations were based on the prayer of the blind man who called out to Jesus for help as he approached Jericho (Luke 18:38). Whoever turns to The Jesus Prayer and prays it with their whole heart and mind and soul is admitting that they are in need and that they are spiritually blind, blinded by the sin and selfishness that only Jesus can cure. The purpose of the prayer is to express this need by repeating it continuously, but in such a gentle way that it leads into the deep interior stillness where one can be totally open to the healing power of the One who 'makes all things new'.

The Philokalia explains an ancient tradition that is believed to go all the way back to St. John Climacus and his disciple St. Hesychius of Sinai; This holds that if The Jesus Prayer is recited with the practice of deep rhythmic breathing it helps the believer enter into the deep inner peace that is at the heart of hesychasm. A later practice involved using a sort of rosary made of knotted cord to count the number of times the prayer is recited. This counting has no significance other than to facilitate the gentle concentration that helps put 'the old man' to rest so that 'the new man who rose from the tomb on the first Easter day can become the center of the heart's attention. It is important to realize that the use of The Jesus Prayer with or without rhythmic breathing or a rosary is not some sort of esoteric technique or magic mantra that invariably leads a person to true contemplation. It is merely a well-tried traditional means of prayer that helps keep the heart in the deep interior stillness where it can best remain intent on the God who alone calls a person onward to the ever-deepening experience of authentic mystical contemplation.

The fact that various forms of group prayer have led many serious searchers through spiritual adolescence and through the same desert that enveloped me is one of the main reasons for the recent revival of interest in The Jesus Prayer, as well as other forms of "pure prayer" derived from the Desert Fathers. People seem to find in the great spiritual masters of the past what the spiritual masters of the present are unable to give them. Perhaps I can be excused, therefore, if I look a little more deeply into "The Prayer of the Heart" and what the earliest Desert Fathers have to say about it.

42

In extremis

The monk who taught my brother to use The Jesus Prayer when no other form of prayer could help him, said that even this would prove too long when the going got tougher. He told him the story of how he had been enveloped in thick clouds whilst playing alone on Dartmoor as a boy. Although he wasn't far from home, he knew the moor well enough to know that one false move could easily plunge him to his death in the treacherous mires that surrounded him. The clouds became darker and darker as evening set in, and torrential rain soaked him to the skin. He was cold and frightened, and began to cry out continuously, "Help! Help! Help!" When he was at the end of his tether a passing shepherd heard his cries, wrapped him in a warm sheepskin and carried him safely home.

The monk told my brother that when you are in desperate need you don't waste time on irrelevant words. You cry out in as few words as possible to express your heart's deepest and most urgent desire. And when you do that, you have never before been so fully at one with yourself. Never before has your body, with all its feelings and emotions, and your mind, with all its powers of understanding and reasoning, been so united as one in a heart that cries out to be heard.

When young monks first arrived to seek God in the desert, they were full of enthusiasm for the search ahead of them. But when the fervour that had led them there in the first place suddenly left them, they found themselves alone in an inner desert surrounded by darkness and desolation. That itself was bad enough, but when the "demons" began to taunt and tempt them as never before it was time to cry out for help. Like the young boy stranded on the moor, they were taught to embody their needs in a single word or phrase. It might be a word like 'help', or 'mercy', repeated over and over again, to express their utter powerlessness to help themselves and their need of the only One who could. The great Abbot Macarius told his disciples to say simply, "To the rescue."

If that young boy on the moor had known who the shepherd was, and known that he was close at hand, he would certainly have called out to him by name. This is how The Jesus Prayer was first born in the desert, as young monks in their direst need called out for help to the Good Shepherd by name. Sometimes "The Prayer of the Heart" would become a phrase or a short sentence, to express at one and the same time the monk's need and the One he needed more than anyone else. So it would become "Jesus help," or "Jesus mercy," or "Come, Lord Jesus."

Although all the monks would experience moments of intense crisis when their pain would be all but unbearable, and no more than a word or two would be needed to express their desperation, these moments would pass. Then they would have to experience a less intense but even more threatening ordeal that would test their resolve to the limit, precisely because it would go on and on, year in and year out.

It was the dreaded "acedia," an extreme form of spiritual weariness and depression that all the monks had to learn to live with if they would live for long in the desert. Now the simple form of prayer that had supported them in extremis was expanded to support them in what would easily have become an intolerable spiritual drudgery without it. This is the context in which The Jesus Prayer in its fullest form began to emerge as the monks realized ever more fully that it was, they alone, and their own personal sinfulness, that separated them from the One who had first drawn them into the desert. A phrase like "Jesus have mercy on me a sinner" seemed to say it all, and so it became one of the earliest forms of "The Prayer of the Heart" that was to become so popular for so many in subsequent centuries.

For it is not just the inhabitants of the monastic world, but the inhabitants of the secular world too, who fall a prey to the dreaded "acedia." Many of them found that the prayer which kept the monks on course when they were in danger of falling by the wayside helped them too in their hour of need. It certainly helped me, as it did my brother, but it was a surprise to learn how it helped my parents also when "acedia" began to seep into their marriage, and no other form of prayer could help them.

43

Preaching to the converted

When my parents first came to visit me in my monastic seclusion, I was full of enthusiasm for the Desert Fathers, and of their spiritual wisdom that had saved my prayer life from disaster. I'd never discussed anything of any depth with my parents before, but I was so full of what I'd been reading that I couldn't contain myself. At last, I could teach them something for a change. I reminded them of how my brother Peter had been helped by The Jesus Prayer, when he found himself in a spiritual depression that guaranteed the most miserable Christmas the rest of the family could remember. I was beginning to explain to them that The Jesus Prayer was but one example of what the Desert Fathers called "The Prayer of the Heart," when I had the distinct impression that they knew exactly what I was talking about.

I knew that Gus helped them in many ways over the years, but I didn't know that he'd taught them about "The Prayer of the Heart." Gus, as he was known to the family, had known my mother for years before she was married, and before he became Dom Aiden Williams, a member of the Benedictine community at Belmont, where he later became Abbot. When their marriage was going through a particularly difficult patch, Gus told them that spiritual weariness and depression was as common in the monastic life as it was in married life. The first monks called it "acedia" and turned to "The Prayer of the Heart" as the main means of keeping their plough on course, when it seemed pointless to plough any longer in the desert. It prevented them from looking backwards, or any way other than forwards towards the One who seemed at times to be no more than a mirage conjured up by their imaginations.

He told them about St. Benedict and how he was helped by the Desert Fathers, and particularly by John Cassian, who had lived in the Egyptian desert for years. There he had known many of the great abbots personally and had written down their pro-found spiritual teaching for posterity. It was from Abbot Isaac that he learned a form of The Prayer of the Heart that could not only help and support a person in times of despondency and depression, but at all times, both within and outside set times for prayer. The formula was simple: "Oh God, come to my aid. O Lord, make haste to help me." Abbot Isaac made it clear that, although this formula had been used from earliest times by the Desert Fathers, it was taught only to those who were ready to receive it. It is not the sort of spiritual fare to set before the proud and arrogant, who think they can manage quite well for themselves, thank you very much?

Believers in positive thinking, who have learned to believe only in themselves, won't be very impressed by a spirituality that grows out of the experience of one's utter weakness and unconditional need for God. That's why those who readily take to this form of prayer have usually suffered in one way or the other, and for long enough to make them realize their desperate need for the only One who can help them. Other lengthier forms of prayer have usually proved too elaborate for them, or they have long since passed beyond them. When you are so acutely aware of your need that you don't care a fig what others think of you, you're not ashamed to turn in all humility to the God who can enter only into those who "know their need of him."

My father opened his prayer book to show me a quotation from John Cassian that he had written down to help remind him of the words of Abbot Isaac on how to use his Prayer of the Heart, taken from the Psalms. You must continually recite it in your heart, whatever work you are doing, or office you are holding, or journey you are undertaking; in adversity that you may be delivered, and in prosperity that you may be preserved. You should be so moulded by the constant use of it that when sleep comes you are still considering it so that you become accustomed to repeating it even in your sleep. When you wake let it be the first thing to come into your mind, let it anticipate all your waking thoughts. When you rise from your bed let it send you down on your knees, and thence send you forth to your work and business and let it follow you about all day.

I went back to my cell that night, not pleased, not impressed, but angry that my parents were yet again one step ahead of me. I was so angry that I knelt by my bed and prayed for help. "Oh God, come to my aid. O Lord make haste to help me." But all that did was to pour oil on to the flames and keep the fire smoldering for the rest of the night!

44

The prayer for all times

My mother discovered The Prayer of the Heart without either the inspiration or the help of the Desert Fathers, or anyone else for that matter. In fact, she didn't even know what it was until she'd been using it for years. She thought she knew only one form of prayer that she'd been taught as a young girl. That's why she thought she'd never really grown up spiritually. In fact, she'd outgrown all forms of prayer that couldn't support her on the mystic way into which she had been led without ever realizing it.

The only form of prayer she knew embraced almost every other form of prayer, had she only known it. It had guided her from the foothills to the heights without her ever realizing that she had been going anywhere. That's why you rarely find spiritual arrogance or pride in someone whose spiritual ascent has been made thanks to the Rosary. They may begin by just learning to say the individual prayers and understanding their meaning. Then in time they learn how to recite them in such a way that all the inner senses are sedated except those that are needed to meditate on the individual mysteries. Meditating gradually turns into loving, as the most lovable human being the world has ever known is seen doing the most human things in the world with such love and being hated to death for it. When this happens the beads are no longer counted, the prayers no longer said, only a few spontaneous words are needed to express the feelings that now begin to overflow for the One whose love surpasses all understanding. Then words gradually give way to moments of profound contemplative stillness.

But this honeymoon period of prayer soon comes to an end when the insatiable desire for love unlimited reaches out beyond the human feelings and emotions that would inevitably limit it. Before these believers can follow the heart's pure and insatiable desire for God they have to be purified in the dry and arid desert in which they now find themselves. This is where "The Prayer of the Heart" comes to the rescue. It is the prayer that helps keep the heart's deepest desire on course, when the feelings and emotions that are left behind do nothing but generate distractions that hinder the journey where previously they had helped.

When this happened to my mother, she found herself counting her beads once more and reciting the prayers she'd recited before. But now she didn't meditate on them as she had done then, nor did she even try to meditate on the mysteries that had moved her in the past. She merely used the recitation of the rosary to suffocate the distractions that would otherwise have overwhelmed her, while at the same time helping her deepest desire to remain fixed on God.

In time she discovered that she no longer found it helpful to recite each prayer in full; a word, a phrase or a sentence taken from them was more than enough to help keep her on course. It might be the phrase "Glory be to God," or "Thy will be done," or simply the name of Jesus. Sometimes she would use the beads, sometimes she wouldn't, but she would always hold them in her hands out of habit, because it seemed to help her. Then, depending on her prevailing spiritual needs, she turned to other short prayers, or ejaculations, as St. Augustine first called them. These were prayers she'd learned as a girl like "Sacred Heart of Jesus, I put my trust in you", or "Jesus mercy, Mary help."

44 - The prayer for all times

When her spiritual desert became particularly testing she turned to her old friend Abbot Williams for help. He told her that he couldn't have advised her better than she'd advised herself. He explained the meaning and purpose of "The Prayer of the Heart" as used by the Desert Fathers, that she'd discovered for herself through saying the Rosary. He told her that some people prefer to call it "The Prayer of Naked Faith," because despite the impression given by its name there is no feeling in these short prayers for a long time to come. And when they do rise with feeling it is usually out of a sense of desperation in the pray-er, who feels helpless and hopeless before the God whose absence seems to mock them in their hour of need.

Abbot Williams had just finished a tour of Italian hermitages to research a book he was writing and found that the most popular form of personal prayer was the Rosary, precisely because it could be adapted to suit and satisfy every phase and stage of the spiritual journey. He ended up at San Giovanni Rotundo, where he visited Padre Pio and found that he was virtually inseparable from the Rosary that supported his mystical life more than any other form of prayer. My mother needed no more encouragement to continue her prayer life as it had started, with the same beads that were in her hands when it ended.

Chapter 45

In perfect harmony

Although I'd known Abbot Williams for years, as a friend of the family, it was only when he visited me at our house of studies that I talked to him for the first time about the spiritual life. He told me he'd recently visited Fonte Colombo, one of our hermitages in Italy, where St. Francis had written his Rule. He said that when the lights were turned on for compline he was struck by a quotation, attributed to St. Bernadine of Siena, written in letters of gold above the choir stalls. Although it was written in Latin, even I was able to understand it, so I didn't have to disgrace myself by asking him to translate it for me. The words were these: "*Si cor non orat, in vanum lingua laborat.*" "If the heart does not pray, the tongue labours in vain."

The Abbot said that if he had his way these words would be written in the choir of every convent, every friary, and every monastery so that nobody would ever forget that words are only means to help support and sustain the heart, as it endeavours to open itself 'and remain open to God. Any form of prayer will inevitably degenerate into meaningless babble if it becomes anything other than a means by which the human heart is raised to remain open to the divine. There is no perfect form of personal prayer in of itself he insisted, but only different forms of prayer that are perfect for as long as they help a person to remain open to God. Words, he said, are only

Chapter 45 - In perfect harmony

means. You should feel free to pick and choose at all times and use whatever helps you to do "the one thing necessary."

He quoted Dom John Chapman, whose spiritual letters I was reading at the time. He had been Abbot Williams' spiritual director when he was a young monk. He said he never tired of saying, "Pray as you can, not as you can't." And if you find a spiritual director who insists that you should pray as you can't, look for another who helps you to pray as you can, not as he can.

When I asked him to recommend some short prayers that others have found helpful in the spiritual desert in which I found myself, he was at first reluctant. When I pressed him he defended his reticence by saying that he felt everyone should be free to choose what prayer best sums up their own personal relationship to God at the precise moment when they try to open their hearts to him. After all, that's why "The Prayer of the Heart" was so named. So prayer time in the desert is not the time to borrow prayers from someone else, unless they express what you want to say better than any words of your own. However, he said, when a person has travelled for long in the desert, whatever formulas they do use are generally reducible to two, first described by the great Abbot Macarius.

Macarius was a contemporary of St Antony who founded the first monastic community in the remote and inhospitable desert of Scetis. He used to say, "There is no need to lose yourself in speaking, it is enough to say 'Lord, as you will'. If the combat presses hard say, "Lord to the rescue." God knows what is needful to you and will have pity on you. Abbot Williams pointed out that these short prayers echoed the prayer of Jesus himself in Gethsemane when he surrendered himself again and again to the Father's will, though he was savaged by terrible temptations from which he asked for deliverance.

But the ultimate prayer, he said, that gradually takes root in the heart after years of travelling in the spiritual wilderness is the final prayer that Jesus made on the cross. "Father, into your hands I commend my spirit." This prayer gradually supersedes all others, not only in times of temptation, but at all times. It is the ultimate act of faith and trust because it involves the most perfect and unconditional offering of one's whole being to God.

God can act perfectly only in those who perfectly give themselves over to him. When the heart's desire genuinely begins to pray in harmony with this prayer then it is the greatest prayer that anyone can ever make, and it will herald the greatest work that God can ever perform, in those who perfectly surrender themselves to him. I knew I was far from the place where I could make this prayer with all my heart, so I asked Abbot Williams to lead me there. But despite his best efforts, and my best intentions, my heart is still far from the perfect harmony it desires with the prayer it would like to make more than any other.

46

An oasis in the desert

Despite his obvious learning, Abbot Williams was such a good and simple man that it seemed the most natural thing in the world to open myself to him as I never opened myself to anyone before. I told him about a new and exciting development in my prayer life that I never told to another living soul. I felt that if none of the priests I'd approached in the student house seemed to understand the desert I had been going through for the last eighteen months or more, they'd hardly understand the oases that I'd come to at the end of it. At first these oases refreshed me but briefly, before I found myself back in the desert again, thirsting more than ever.

The first oases were hardly noticeable. It was just that amidst all the dryness and aridity, that made me feel prayer was pointless, I occasionally became aware of a subtle strengthening power. It enabled me to push on with a semblance of the moral fibre that had been falling apart in the preceding months. Then it gradually began to dawn on me that something was happening on a level far deeper than the dissipating distractions that never left me for a moment. The conviction that strength was being received was eventually confirmed by the subtle awareness of a gentle form of inner recollection that was not self-imposed. It came and went at will, not, however, at my will, for I would have willed it all the time. At first it felt almost exactly the same as those natural mystical experiences that had aroused my sense of the sacred in the past, but it was not triggered off by any form of external stimulus. It made me feel that I was not alone after all, nor had I been alone despite the months in the wilderness.

Then on several occasions all subtlety was cast aside, and the gentle inner recollection became profoundly absorbing, so that I didn't even want to move from where I was and could do so only with difficulty. The deep inner peace that enveloped me ebbed and flowed with varying degrees of intensity. Shortly before Abbot Williams had come to visit me, these experiences that had left me for a time returned more powerfully than ever before. I could only explain them to him in the light of two experiences that I'd had at school. Like so many other adolescents I'd been hungry for exotic experiences that would enable me to glimpse another, more exciting world that transcended my boring boarding school existence with all its drabness and drudgery.

On one occasion I was using a bottle of Dabitoff to remove custard stains from my Sunday blazer, when I was attracted to the smell of the solvent. When I'd finished dabbing it off my blazer, I started dabbing it on my handkerchief so that I could savor the smell more intensely. Three sniffs later I was on the floor of the locker room, totally absorbed in a strange stupor. After this my 'experiments' were confined to the dormitory after lights out, until I was discovered. I was referred to the chemistry master, who warned me that I could well end up even more brain-dead than my escapades suggested if I continued with my lunacy. Although I'd found these dangerous experiments enjoyable, they were nothing to compare with what I experienced when the nurse pumped me full of pethidine before I had my tonsils out. I knew then what nirvana was like, without all the ascetic efforts that were supposed to precede it.

Despite my embarrassment, Abbot Williams knew exactly what I was trying to say and assured me that, far from being an unusual development in prayer life, my experience merely confirmed what should be the norm, not the abnormal. He told me that the deep interior peace that had enveloped me was one of the first signs that led the earliest monks to believe that the presence of God was beginning to draw them to himself. In order to describe these spiritual oases, they had to borrow the word "apatheia" from the Stoics and Christianize it. Then it came to mean the inner peace that progressively permeates the whole being, as the passions are purified and pacified by God working through the personal endeavor that is perfected in prayer.

He warned me, however, that spiritual oases have an uncanny knack of drying up just when you think you can rely on them. Then once again one must travel on in the desert that comes alive with what the Desert Fathers called 'demons', who have to be defeated before peace can return and return permanently. These were indeed prophetic words that I found out to my cost in the barren years that lay ahead of me.

Chapter 47

Hide-and-seek

I was busily boring the class to death with stories of the Desert Fathers when one teenage girl started chanting, "What about the Desert Mothers!" I pretended not to hear her because I didn't know what to say. Of course, I'd known that many women had felt called to the desert, but I didn't know much about them and, truth to tell, I couldn't name one of them.

I spent that evening in the library and could not believe my luck when I discovered that one of the most important of the Desert Mothers was called Melanie, a name she shared with the girl who'd been taunting me that very morning. Melanie was a wealthy heiress married to Valerius Maximus, prefect of Rome. When her husband died, she gave away all her money and went to Jerusalem where she founded a double monastery. In 382 a distinguished visitor stayed at that monastery and came under her influence. His name was Evagrius. He was both a friend and a pupil of St. Basil, St. Gregory of Nyssa, and St. Gregory Nazianzus, and was the greatest mystical theologian of his day. After months of indecision, it was Melanie who finally persuaded him to embrace the monastic life in the Egyptian desert. At first, he learned all he could about the spiritual life from two great masters, Macarius the Great and Abbot Ammonius. Then he himself began to have an enormous influence on

Chapter 47 - Hide-and-seek

his fellow monks through his writings and his profound mystical theology.

The first monks were for the most part simple unlettered men. The great St. Antony was a peasant farmer, Pachomius an ordinary soldier and Macarius a camel driver. They didn't see themselves as monks as we understand them today, but as lay-men who simply wanted to live a more radical Christian life "far from the madding crowd." Their spiritual wisdom was handed on by word of mouth and only written down much later. Evagrius didn't so much record their wisdom as assimilate it into his own spiritual life, and thence into his masterly, mystical synthesis.

He was the first to apply the Greek words "acedia" and "apatheia" to the spiritual life of the early monks. "Acedia" was used to describe the spiritual weariness and fatigue that could lead the monks into the direst desolation that bordered on despair. The word "apatheia" describes the inner calm and peace when the passions are pacified, at least for a time, before the final victory over the "demons." Then a permanent peace that surpasses all understanding would raise the victor to paroxysms of joy that could only be contained in ecstasy. The combination of his great learning and the wisdom he gained in the desert, enabled Evagrius to produce the first great spiritual synthesis that has had an enormous effect on Christian spirituality ever since.

It was developed and deepened in subsequent centuries by other spiritual writers, finally finding its fullest expression in the writings of the great Carmelite mystics. If St. John of the Cross explored more fully than ever before the nature and meaning of "acedia" in his *Dark Night of the Soul*, then St. Teresa of Avila did likewise for "apatheia" in her masterwork, *Interior Castle*. Though they used different words and symbols to express their profound teaching, it is essentially the same as that of Evagrius.

Prolonged periods of absence experienced in "acedia" and brief moments of presence experienced through "apatheia" always characterize a person's relationship with God in the journey through their spiritual desert or 'dark night of the soul'. When the desert seems totally desolate, they turn to The Prayer of the Heart that begs for help, for perseverance and for patience to journey on, despite the "acedia" that threatens to lead them to despair. When unexpected oases give temporary refreshment, then their prayer bursts out into thanksgiving, praise and glory to the One who has led them there. No matter how self-centred a person is when they are led into the desert, the One who led them there will eventually make them selfless through his mysterious game of 'hide-and-seek'. Only then will the peace that surpasses understanding surpass all they've ever hoped for and do so permanently.

When I told my taunter the story of her illustrious namesake she was not at all impressed. "If I was a wealthy heiress," she said, "I'm darned if I'd give up everything just to live in a desert searching for some sort of peace that I can't even understand when I find it." There have been times when the words of that girl who taunted me in the past have taunted me again, as I struggled for meaning in my own spiritual desert. Was it really all worth it for the peace that surpasses understanding? I know the answer when it possesses me, but I'm not so sure when it leaves me where it found me.

48

The Rambo within

Some people can watch horror after horror on the television without turning a hair. But I meet more and more people who just have to switch off, because they can't take it anymore. A neighbour of mine admitted that she finds it all but impossible to watch the news any longer. We didn't have a television when I was a student, but the papers were bad enough. I thought that the war to end all wars meant that there'd be peace in the world, at least in my lifetime, but I was wrong. There might have been peace of a sort in my part of the world, but there seemed to be more wars than ever in the rest of the world.

The Vietnamese students who were studying with us told stories that gave me nightmares, stories of the killing fields in their own country. They had seen their own parents shot in front of them, relatives tortured before their eyes, and countless numbers of their own people bombed, and burned alive with napalm, by the 'friendly fire' of those who came to liberate them.

The prayer that was dark enough before became even darker when the pictures of the terrible inhumanity of my fellow human beings flashed and flickered through my mind. The retreat master whom I spoke to said that's exactly how it was with Jesus as he tried to pray in Gethsemane. He said it was traditionally believed that Jesus sweated with blood, not just at the thought of what irrational human beings would do to his physical body the next day, but at what they would do to his Mystical Body until the end of time, despite all he would do for them. He told me that I could at least take comfort from experiencing in some small way what Jesus had to experience in a far greater way when he cried out in prayer to be delivered from his mental torture.

What the retreat master said helped me, but I received even greater help from Paul, one of the Vietnamese students. He told me how he had played "Rambo" in the jungle for two years, seeking revenge on those who had mutilated and massacred most of his family. Then something he did, that he could not speak about made him realize that what was in those men who murdered his family was also in him. He told me that he came to understand that the real war to end all wars must be fought within ourselves, and so he left "the Patriots" to seek a place where the real war could be won. The evil in the world, he insisted, does not come from the jungle where he used to hide, or the sea where he used to refresh himself, or from the sky that used to speak to him at night of the peace and beauty of the One he had all but forgotten in his anger. It comes from within a sick and sullied human heart.

Paul's words confirmed even more powerfully what a visiting missionary had said to me when I told him I wanted to leave to solve the problems of the world single-handed. The problems in my own personal world had to be faced first, the problems that lurked deep down within me, so deep that I had no idea they were there at all, never mind how deeply embedded they were in the nether regions of my personality.

I was able to persevere in prayer thanks to all the encouragement I received, though it was a daily Gethsemane. If I was left to myself I would have avoided it and would never have known something of the consolations that Jesus experienced in his Gethsemane. At first, I thought they were given as a sort of reward for my perseverance, and in part I suppose they were, but they were much more than that. They not only drew me up and out of myself where I forgot all the troubles of the world for a time, but they enabled me to see what was in me that caused and added to those troubles.

Paul told me that the same had happened to him and explained why. When all that is within our hearts and minds is lost for a time in the contemplation of God, the wily old egotist who rules us forgets to keep guard on the dungeons within. When this happens the dark side of what we really are escapes and emerges into the light of our conscious minds, where it has to be seen and faced for what it is. As the experience of the grandeur of what God is subsides, the grubbiness of what we are rises up. So light is always followed by darkness. But when forgiveness is sought for what is seen and faced, it is always given by the love that draws out more and more from the depths till all is seen and then forgiven. Then the war to end all wars is won and peace reigns where turmoil reigned before.

There will be no permanent peace on earth until this peace is won in everyone. Simplistic as this may sound, it's even more simplistic to believe in a permanent peace without the personal peace that can alone sustain it.

49

Spiritual paternity

All papers, even Catholic papers were considered a corrupting influence during my novitiate. As a result, I was so hungry for newsprint that when they were restored to me at our student house I began to devour everything, even the editorials! But what had initially lit up my darkness soon became darkness itself, when all the world's woes began to crowd in on me in the prayer time that had already become all doom and gloom.

Prolonged periods of solitude forced me to face the sea of troubles that were washed up in my mind from all over the world I had left for what began to look increasingly like a life of spiritual self-indulgence. A little voice inside me began to say, "You are running away from reality because you can't face it."

Everything came to a head when one of our visiting missionaries gave us a talk about the hideous cancer of apartheid that was eating the heart and soul out of the country where he had been working for over ten years. He told us in detail about the Sharpeville massacre where scores of black African men, women and children had been brutally cut down, shot in the back as they ran away from the security forces, who pleaded self-defense! He said that he'd met with one of the leaders of the ANC, who told him that violence was

49 - Spiritual paternity

now inevitable for he could see no other way to gain the justice and freedom that was the birthright of his people.

I was so moved by what he said that I told him I wanted to leave there and then to do something for the problems of the world that haunted me in my solitary prayer. He would have none of it. "How can you solve the world's problems," he said, "when you are part of the problem?" He told me to give up reading about the world's problems for Lent so that nothing could prevent me from facing my own. He explained that my 'hidden years' were a preparation for helping to solve the problems of the world by first facing my own, and then turning to the only One who can solve them.

For if we do not go out with at least something of 'the answer' within us then we go out with empty hearts and minds, to add our own problems to those we ought to be trying to solve. The missionary said that seven years was little enough time to prepare myself. The great St. Antony spent twenty years in solitude before his would-be disciples broke down the gates of the old fortress where he had incarcerated himself so that he could become their spiritual father.

In his life of the great founder of monasticism, St Athanasius shows how spiritual paternity is the consummation of a life of solitary prayer when the self-knowledge that leads to spiritual wisdom enables the monk to become a spiritual father, not just to his fellow monks but to his fellow human beings. He describes how, towards the end of his life, Antony left his monastic seclusion to go back into the world where his teaching and preaching achieved a success that would have been quite impossible without the solitude that preceded it.

I was reminded of that missionary and of what he taught me all those years ago when the ANC leader he had told me about was released from prison in 1990. He had spent not seven or even twenty years, but twenty-seven years in solitude, where he learned that there is an alternative to violence when violence has been defeated in oneself. If you want to see the most perfect embodiment of spiritual paternity in the modern world, look no further than this man. He is for me a most saintly man; remade in the image and likeness of the Man he met in his solitude.

This is the man who has been able to bring the peace and unity that Jesus prayed for, not just to his own family, his own people, or his own religion, but to a whole nation that was rampant and rotting with racism. Let's hope that seeing is believing for a world in desperate need of what one man did for his own fellow countrymen because of what was first done to him.

50

The spiritual combat

Brother Taurus was a man with the best of intentions but with a terrible temper that made him impossible to live with. After he had fallen out with his family, he went to Tarsus to be apprenticed to a tailor. When he had frightened away half his customers the tailor had to send him away before he lost the other half.

It was then that Taurus decided to do something about his temper before it did for him. He went into the desert and found a monastery in which he could live while he came to terms with his affliction. In less than a year the monks found his temper so impossible that he had to leave. They gave him a fine set of earthenware pots and plates, a large jug of goat's milk and enough food for a month. Then they helped him find a cave in which to live the life of a hermit. At last, he thought he could come to terms with his temper because there was no one there to try him.

It was when he was trying to light the fire that he overturned the jug and lost all his milk. Before he could control himself, he picked up the jug and smashed it against the side of the cave. The pots went the next day and the plates the following day. Brother Taurus cursed and swore but there was no longer anywhere for him to go to hide from the affliction that would have gone with him anyway. At last, he had to face in solitude what he'd never faced before. It was there that he finally learned that the trouble with the world he had run away from was not "other people," as Sartre said, but with himself. If he wanted to live in peace with others, he must first find it within himself"

St Catherine of Siena said, "The trouble with the world is me!" It was a truth that she learned for herself in blood, sweat and tears in her solitude, not in a desert but in her own home, in what she called "the house of self-knowledge." It takes a saint to see a truth clearly when pride and prejudice prevent the rest of us from seeing it. The evils of the world that we hear about daily on our radios or see on our television screens are but the outward expressions of the evil that is within us all.

Yet arrogant human beings find it offensive when they are told that the source of the world's woes can be found within them. They like to think that they have no part in them, that the problems exist out there in a place where they can be dealt with by the expertise and endeavour of Homo sapiens. That is why Schumacher pointed out in his book *Small Is Beautiful* that "Although people go on clamouring out for solutions, they become angry when they are told that the restoration of society must come from within, not from without." Simplistic it may seem to the clumsy, cluttered mind of Homo arrogans, but it is nevertheless true. There will never be peace and harmony in the human world until there is first peace and harmony in the human heart. This has been the consistent teaching of the great philosophers and religious thinkers from the beginning.

All the great mystics have discovered the hard way what Job meant when he said that man's life on earth is a continual war, a war that has to be waged within. Pope John XXIII's bedside reading was *The Spiritual Combat*, from which he drew his inspiration. This man of peace and compassion only became so through many inner battles that he fought and lost, as he explained in the book *Journal of a*

50 - The spiritual combat

Soul. It is only after losing battle after battle in the spiritual combat that a person finally learns that "the war to end all wars" will never be won without help and strength that is quite beyond one's own resources.

This was the lesson that St. Paul finally learned. He actually thanked God for his weakness because it enabled him to realize that without God he couldn't win a single battle with himself. For St. Paul, even sinfulness can become a steppingstone to sanctity when it forces a person to turn again and again to the only One who can help him. The way to inner peace is paved with spiritual failures and dogged by defeat after defeat. If victory ever comes it will come through the humility of the broken warrior, who begs for the help and strength that he finally realizes only God can give.

No politician, no diplomat did more for peace in her day than did St Catherine of Siena. Nor will anyone do more for peace in our day than those who have the courage to look within, as she did, and with God's help fight first with themselves for what they want to bring to others.

51

True wisdom

Charlie had been captured by the Vietcong, put into solitary confinement for months on end, and then interrogated for days as part of their brain-washing technique. He was one of four Vietnamese students who stayed with us in the sixties. Two of the others had seen their parents shot in front of them, the third spent two years hiding in the jungle in fear for his life. For the first few weeks after his arrival Charlie had been the life and soul of the party, a lovable extrovert who was popular with all the students. Then he suddenly went into his shell and never came out of it.

The technique of brainwashing had been perfected before the Second World War in the Soviet Union, where they first discovered how human beings could be broken by merely placing them in solitude. Stripped of everything that could distract them from facing the seedy and sordid self that emerges in solitude, a person's security was shattered long before the interrogator began his work. In the shows trials at the end of the thirties the world saw for the first time how a new man could be totally reconstructed from the old man according to the designs of political expediency by a skilled interrogator. Charlie had been broken and reset. He had denounced his country, his family and his faith long before "friendly forces" had freed him. They freed his body but they could do nothing to free his mind.

51 - True wisdom

There is no virtue in prolonged solitude for its own sake, only danger. The Desert Fathers were adamant that nobody should leave human habitation for the desert unless they were led there by the same Spirit that led Jesus into the desert. The monk would have to face trials and temptations as Jesus did in his solitude, but these trials and temptations would come from the 'demons' within that were never in Jesus.

The danger of seeing too much too quickly was avoided by building a lifestyle in which manual work, the study of the Scriptures, the recitation of the Psalms and solitary prayer were balanced under the guidance of an experienced father. As what had been hidden gradually began to surface during his solitude, the monk was inevitably shocked and shattered by the arrogance and pride that had ruled him before. It is a humiliating and humbling experience to see oneself laid bare, and to experience one's utter weakness and one's powerlessness to do anything about it.

In the technique of brain-washing this is the moment when the interrogator stamps his own false security on to the insecurity of his victim, so that the victim begins to identify with the interrogator and with his ideals and standards. Now the interrogator becomes God and begins the process of re-creating his victim into whatever image and likeness he wants.

When, in his solitude, the monk begins to see himself as he really is, he too experiences his own utter weakness and in-ability to help himself. This is the moment when his spiritual father teaches him how to turn to Someone else in his need. This is why The Prayer of the Heart, that is first uttered by the monk in his solitude, is a cry for help as he realizes that he cannot help himself.

God cannot resist the *cri de coeur* that rises from the weakness of someone who genuinely knows their need of him. God's power works most perfectly in weakness. That is the great secret of the spiritual life that the monk discovers in his hour of greatest need. Now it is God, not some sadistic interrogator, who begins the work of destroying the old man so that a new man can be formed in the image of the New Man who rose from the tomb on the first Easter day. This profound transformation takes years rather than months and involves moments of deep depression followed by profound peace, and sometimes ecstatic joy as God's work is brought to completion.

The first men and women who fled into the desert were not religious but lay people urged by a holy impatience to seek the transformation they desired as quickly as possible. All serious Christians are called to this same transformation in a spiritual desert into which the Spirit leads all who take up a serious life of prayer. Here and here alone will they learn true self-knowledge, the knowledge of their own utter weakness and the true wisdom that makes them turn as never before to the only One who can make them new.

52

From stumbling blocks to stepping stones

If I was not dyslexic I would have joined the Jesuits, but I knew they would turn me down the moment they found out I did not have a single O Level, never mind an A. So, I joined the Franciscans instead, not because they would take anyone, but because my brother who preceded me had such brilliant academic credentials that nobody bothered to question mine.

They soon realized their mistake when they heard me stumbling through the readings in the refectory and stuttering my way through the recitation of the Psalms and the long Latin lessons in the choir. The novitiate was not supposed to be a heaven on earth, but it was hell on earth for me, because my little problem quadrupled the statutory humiliations that all had to endure.

An aunt of mine sent me a proverb for my birthday, written in a large Gothic script and framed in formica so it could be hung above my bed. I bunged it into the bin before the others could see it, but I can still remember the words: "Make all your stumbling blocks into stepping stones, and they'll carry you across the most treacherous of torrents." The word 'Yuk' had not been invented in those days, so I could not use it to express how I felt about a Victorian epigram that nevertheless contained an important biblical truth I had yet to discover.

I would have liked to have explained to my fellow novices why I had more than my fair share of stumbling blocks, but I didn't know myself. As I could not turn to anyone else for comfort, I had no choice but to turn to God. The novitiate would have been a complete waste of time for me if it had not created whole acres of space each evening in which I could seek the solace I needed from the only One who could give it.

Thanks to the school spiritual director I knew what to do and what to say in the time for which the others were sadly never prepared. The first fervour that fermented in my prayer every evening convinced me that I was right to stay at the place that I always wanted to leave every morning. I packed my bags several times before Matins when my first fervor finally fizzled out, and the night time became even worse than the day.

If a visiting Carmelite priest hadn't promised me that God reveals himself in a very special and personal way to those who persevere in prayer through darkness and depression, I would have done much more than merely packed my bags. I think I'd probably have gone anyway if my brother had not made it before me and been waiting for me at the other side of 'purgatory'.

The student house was not heaven on earth but it was not far short of it, compared with what I'd been through. If only the prayer that I once found so easy and so enjoyable had returned, I would have been happy enough, but it did not. If there was not something about that Carmelite priest that made me believe he knew what he was talking about, I would have given up prayer and turned to the 'fleshpots' for comfort, though there were not too many of them in our student house Then quite out of the blue what he promised began to happen.

With very little warning the prayer that had been destroyed by dis-

52 - From stumbling blocks to stepping stones

tractions became more and more absorbing as all that had been dissipated before became riveted on something or Some One, whose presence became all-engrossing. Then all that was absorbed was suddenly raised to higher and higher degrees of intensity. It was as if my mind and all that was in it had become a lift or an elevator that was responding to a powerful other-worldly force that raised it to different levels of mystical awareness where it remained fully engrossed.

The Prayer of the Heart that before had only cried out for help, now cried out in joy and praise and in thanksgiving for the return in fuller measure of what had been experienced only in lesser measure before. Finally, all words had to be put aside for no words can express the inexpressible. That is why St. Antony said, "You do not pray perfectly until you do not seem to be praying at all." When an ever-fuller union begins to unite those who were separate before, words gradually give way to a still and awe-ful silence.

Despite my reluctance to admit it, I saw for the first time that my auntie's little epigram was right. What I had thought were my greatest stumbling blocks had become stepping stones that led me through a desert of daily drudgery to an oasis that I had never dreamt of before. At last, I found my heaven on earth that I thought would last forever, but no oasis lasts for long "when the well runs dry!"